Myths

&

Mistranslations

By

Jamie Englehart

Myths and Mistranslations
by Jamie Englehart

Published by Whisper Publishing
Copyright © Jamie Englehart
ALL RIGHTS RESERVED

Cover Design: Nate Ebel
First Printing –September 2018
ISBN –ISBN-13:978-1727397215
ISBN-101727397215

NO PART OF THIS BOOK MAY BE REPRODUCED IN ANY FORM, BY PHOTOCOPYING OR BY ANY ELECTRONIC OR MECHANICAL MEANS, INCLUDING INFORMATION STORAGE OR RETRIEVAL SYSTEMS, WITHOUT PERMISSION IN WRITING FROM THE COPYRIGHT OWNER/AUTHOR

Printed in the USA

All Scripture is in NASB unless otherwise stated. Greek and Hebrew from Strong's Concordance and Young's Concordance

DEDICATION

I would like to dedicate this book to my family. First, my wife Wendy Englehart and our children Brittany Rocha and Brandon Englehart, who had to sit in restaurants and homes for hours listening to me discuss and dialogue with others about the things contained in these pages. They have been amazing at allowing me to ask questions to come to conclusions, without judgement, and have been supportive even though it was not always their thing or what they were into. I am proud of each of them and honored to be Wendy's husband, a father and a grandfather to our amazing children and grandchildren.

I also want to dedicate this to all the true "Bereans" that have been in my life through the years who have challenged me to think and study for myself. All the friends, fathers, mothers, brothers, sisters, and son's and daughters who have continually forced me to grow rather then be comfortable with the status quo. I have been a blessed man having you all in my life.

ACKNOWLEDGMENTS

I want to acknowledge several amazing people who were a part of forming my thinking, study, beliefs, and questions through my life. First, my parents, Rev. James & Darlene Englehart, who I drove crazy with questions and who put in me a desire to study and learn. Dr. Fuschia Pickett, a mother in the faith who caused me to ask the right questions and to always be open to present truth and revelation by the Holy Spirit, within proper Scriptural context. Apostle Chuck Clayton, a true father who believed in me and did not try to make me conform to his way of thinking; he was always supportive and confirming, even if he did not have the answer or agree. Dr. Lynn Hiles, who was instrumental in helping give me language for much of what I had studied and believed; one who has been a true friend as well as one of my favorite preachers. Also, Sonia Borisow who proofed, edited and saw to the publishing of this book. Then, last but not least, all of the sons and daughters in the faith who have pulled this information out of me through the years and encouraged me to write it down, so it could be left as part of their inheritance.

FORWARD

In this season, we are probably in one of the greatest reformations since Martin Luther. Information, both good and bad are at our fingertips like never before, with the availability of the Internet. This can be scary to the mind that does not want to be challenged. In this great book, Bishop Jamie Englehart does not necessarily teach you what to think, but simply to think. Traditional mindsets and preconceived ideas that we have been taught by religion, without questioning, are our biggest enemies. Many have hidden behind the clichés and rhetoric of nonbiblical traditions that have become a refuge of lies. It is only the truth that will make you free. If it is not making you free, it is probably not the truth. The sad truth is that many people love darkness more than they love the light. For those of you who love the truth, this book will be an eye-opener.

The quest for truth is truly a journey. Sometimes the truth will make you mad before it makes you free. I simply suggest that you read this with an open mind and allow the Holy Spirit to be the teacher. Grow at your own pace with what you are comfortable with. Different people are at different stages of their journey.

I am reminded of the children of Israel in their wilderness journey. As they left Egypt by the millions, the people at the front of the line would be experiencing something totally different than the people at the back of the line. For instance, when they crossed the Red Sea, the folks at the front of the line were experiencing a baptism in the cloud, while the folks at the back of the line were experiencing baptism in water at the Red Sea. Deliverance is by divine degrees. They were delivered by the blood of the Lamb in Egypt. They were delivered by water at the Red Sea. They were baptized into the cloud at Mt. Sinai. They were sustained by manna in the wilderness, etc. Each stage of the journey was a greater revelation of God and his redemptive plan for them. It was the unfolding of the manifold glory of God. We must not camp out around one truth. We must press for the whole counsel of God.

I can remember as a young man, the first time I realized that the King James Bible was not the only translation that was accurate. As a matter of fact, the more scrolls like the Dead Sea Scrolls, that have been found by archaeologist to compare manuscripts with, the more accurate our translations become. For instance, one of the great shifts in my thinking came when I realized how the King James Bible sometimes translates the word, 'world' it is actually a Greek word that means 'age'. It was a huge paradigm shift for me. I realized, for example in Matthew 24, the end of the world was not the end of a global cosmic collapse but was in fact the end of the age of the Old Covenant. That became a massive shift in my thinking. It really made me realize that we are truly living in the New Covenant of grace. Myths and mistranslations have hindered the church long enough. Buckle your seatbelt and enjoy the journey.

Lynn Hiles Th.D., Ph.D. Author, Itinerant minister
Host of the nationally broadcast television program: "That You Might Have Life."

INTRODUCTION

This book started out as Facebook posts that just kept growing. People began asking me to compile these into a book and have them all together, so here we are. The one thing I want all of you reading this book to know; my purpose in writing these myths is to stimulate dialogue, along with study, and promote the idea that being a good Berean is a positive thing. This is not a theological treatise and each of the points could be a chapter or book alone, but they are a short explanation that will hopefully cause you to think and ask the right questions. So, whether you agree or disagree, I hope these writings will cause you to think for yourself and not just swallow everything you were taught but maybe have not really studied for yourself. My desire is not to indoctrinate you to my way of thinking, but to hopefully get you to think for yourself. Also, I wrote these for people who are at different stages of growth in their journey and tried my best to make it palatable to the many rather than the few. I pray that the Holy Spirit will illuminate these things to you, take you beyond these writings and you would increase in your understanding exponentially. I love and believe in you all, please enjoy.
Thank you and blessings,
Jamie Englehart

Myths & Mistranslations

Myth 1
Lucifer is the devil.

The word (notice I didn't say name) Lucifer is found only one time in the Old English translations of the Bible (KJV and NKJV) in Isaiah 14:12, *How you are fallen from heaven, O Lucifer, son of the morning! How you are cut down to the ground, you who weakened the nations!* It is not found anywhere in the newer translations (NASB, NIV or NLT). The translation of Lucifer in Isaiah 14:12 is 'Morning Star' or 'Shining One' as it is a description of the Hebrew morning star, which most scholars teach was referring to an actual star, called Venus. It is translated in the KJV as Lucifer because the translators used the Latin Vulgate for some of the Old Testament, rather than the actual Hebrew (which is used by the newer translations) and 'Lucifer' is a Latin word describing the 'Morning Star.'

In its historical context, many believe it was referring to King Nebuchadnezzar (the Babylonian king) after his defeat by the Persians, and was a parable dealing with the king's haughtiness towards God (see Daniel) or King Belshazzar, who was the last king of ancient Babylon described in Scripture. Much of Christianity began to teach that the devil and Lucifer were one and the same because of fictional books such as 'Dante's inferno' and Milton's 'Paradise Lost' because they both refer to the devil as 'Lucifer'.

To try and make this mean the devil and his fall from heaven as a former angel, is eisegesis (to read 'into' Scripture what you want it to mean) at best. Jesus, in the New Testament, said, He saw Satan (not Lucifer) fall from Heaven like lightning and that the devil was a liar from the beginning (notice, not an angel who became the devil). The book of Enoch says the angel that caused the rebellion in Heaven was 'Azazel'. So maybe that is why it was not included in the Canon of Scripture and was considered 'myth' just like calling Lucifer the devil. Now, is there a real entity called the devil? Perhaps, I believe so, even though many debate that. Could Isaiah 14 be a metaphor describing demonic and pagan deities and mindsets? Perhaps, but 'Lucifer' is not his name.

Myth #2
Lucifer caused a third of the angels to fall from Heaven with him.

In Myth #1, we not only dealt with the idea of Lucifer not being one of the devil's names, but actually not being a name at all. Instead, it was a description of the Day Star or Morning Star, 'Venus'. It was historically speaking about a Babylonian king. The only time the word 'Lucifer' is found in Scripture is in Isaiah 14. Many have been taught when Lucifer (the devil) caused a rebellion in Heaven, he caused a third of the angels to go with him. Now, this does have merit in Hebrew mysticism and myth as well as the book of Enoch, which by the way, says nothing about anyone called, Lucifer, but does say that the angel Azazel caused a rebellion. This is also a good reason why it was not allowed in the Canon of Scripture: because it was full of myth and mysticism (but it is an interesting read, lol).

This myth comes from the book of Revelation, chapter 12:4, *And his tail swept away a third of the stars of heaven and threw them to the earth. And the dragon stood before the woman who was about to give birth, so that when she gave birth he might devour her child.* This is the only inference of this idea and it is not found anywhere in Scripture. Also, know that the symbolic nature of the book of Revelation must be understood, and we are told at the beginning of Revelation, that the seven stars are the angels of the seven churches, which most believe refers to the leading messengers/pastors and not literal angels. The word translated angels is also 'messengers' which can be men or actual angels. This is the only time it is found in Scripture and to translate it as 'fallen angels' you have to tie quite a few other things together by doing exegetical gymnastics.

Proper study of Scripture teaches that we normally do not build a doctrine on just one verse but need at least 2 or 3 as a witness; plus, there is simply no clear evidence of a third of the angels falling from Heaven, period. Take note also that when God, in the Old Testament, was speaking about stars in the Heavens, He likened it to Abraham's seed. Many scholars believe Revelation could be referring to a third of the nation of Israel being slain and destroyed by the Romans in the forty-two-and-a-half-month war between 67-70 A.D. along with a plethora of other meanings.

Just know that there are a lot of different ideas about all of this, but to come up with most of it, we must read 'in-to' the Scriptures what we want it to mean, rather than read out what is actually written. So, is there an actual devil? Perhaps, I believe so, even though many may debate that. Do we know definitively where he comes from and where his demons come from? No, there is no exact clarity from the Scriptures and if we claim we know, it is theory and conjecture at best. Yet it could be possible, so we don't throw it away, and we also do not teach it as doctrine.

Myth #3
God cannot look on sin.

Many of us have heard and been taught that God cannot look on sin because of His holiness and righteousness. The Scriptures tell us that (God hates sin) and this is true but not because it's kryptonite and weakens Him, but because of its effects on His creation. God knows that sin leads to death and He is light, life, and love. His heart is abundance of life for us. Paul tells us in 2 Corinthians. 5:19, namely, *that God was in Christ reconciling the world to Himself, not counting their trespasses (sins, falling away, missteps, lapses, and slips against them) and He has committed to us the word of reconciliation.* So, if that statement is true, why can't He even look on it?

When we study the Scriptures, what we find is that the only passage that even comes close to saying this is Habakkuk 1:13; *Your eyes are too pure to approve evil, and you cannot look on wickedness with favor. So why do you look with favor on those who deal treacherously?"* In other words, 'Your holiness does not approve of evil' or 'how can you look on it?' So why do you?" The KJV says; *so why do you tolerate them?"* The idea that God cannot look on sin or evil is silly because if true, then He is blind because it is everywhere. Also, if we believe that Jesus and the Father are one and that the incarnation is true, then God looked on sin, touched sin, ate with sinners, and got a pedicure and rubbed down with essential oils from one, lol.

Jesus was called a friend of sinners, so He was obviously looking on sin and it did not weaken Him but instead He, being grace, abounded even more with love, because where sin abounds grace even more abounds. God does not run from sin but towards it. Even in the garden, God did not turn away from Adam and Eve when they sinned, but still came to walk with them, and He even killed an animal and got close enough to clothe them. However, Adam and Eve did turn from God and that is the effects of sin, it brings us under fear and condemnation and we hide from Him; but He does not hide from us. God did not run from Cain after he murdered his brother, but instead got close enough to put His finger on Cain's forehead to leave a mark of protection.

So, God did look on sin, but know that He is not counting or holding it against you, because He took it all away 2,000 years ago and has empowered us to overcome sin by His grace and thru the power of His Indwelling Spirit. Please do not let a sin-conscious teacher or leader make you feel like God has abandoned you when you have messed up, but instead come boldly to the throne of grace to obtain mercy in your time of need.

Myth #4
The devil lives in and rules hell.

Most of us, whether we were church attenders; religious or not, have heard some story of the devil in hell, either ruling or tormenting others. The truth is, it is NOT in the Scriptures and comes more from Dante's 'The Divine Comedy' and the Catholic idea of 'purgatory' as well as Muhammad's 'Night of Ascension'. Dante's along with much of the church's medieval ideas of the devil and hell come more from the Quran and a play and a poem, rather than the Bible.

Now, hell is a real place called 'the grave'. In Greek, it is called 'Hades' and 'Gehenna' which is an actual place called the 'Valley of Hinnom' located just outside Jerusalem. In Hebrew, it is called 'Sheol'. According to Scripture, it was made for the devil and his angels (messengers) and is a place of judgment for them not to give them a place of rule.

The devil does not rule hell, and he has never been there, but will be thrown there some day in the future, according to most traditional teaching. Instead, we are told that he is the prince of the power of the air and walks about on the earth Job 1:6-12, *Now there was a day when the sons of God came to present themselves before the Lord, and Satan also came among them. The Lord said to*

Satan, "From where do you come?" Then Satan answered the Lord and said, "From roaming about on the earth and walking around on it." The LORD said to Satan, "Have you considered My servant Job? For there is no one like him on the earth, a blameless and upright man, fearing God and turning away from evil.: Then Satan answered the Lord, "Does Job fear God for nothing? Have You not made a hedge about him and his house and all that he has on every side? You have blessed the work of his hands, and his possessions have increased in the land. But put forth Your hand now and touch al that he has; he will surely curse You to Your face." Then the Lord said to Satan, "Behold, all that he has is in your power, only do not put forth your hand on him." So, Satan departed from the presence of the Lord. He is walking about seeking whom he may devour. I Peter 5:8, *Be of sober spirit, be on the alert. Your adversary, the devil, prowls around like a roaring lion, seeking someone to devour.*

The devil had the keys of 'death and the grave' which is translated 'hell' but Jesus destroyed his works, Hebrews 2:14, *Therefore, since the children share in flesh and blood, He Himself likewise also partook of the same that through death He might render powerless him who had the power of death, that is, the devil.* Now, Jesus has the keys and authority over 'death and the grave'. The devil along with 'death and hell' will be thrown into the lake of fire and brimstone after the judgement, according to most Orthodox teaching and interpretations of Revelations 20:10-15. Yet, some teachers of eschatology believe it already happened in 70 A.D. which is another thing to study for yourself.

So, is the devil real? Perhaps, I believe so. Is hell a real place? Yes, a few different places. Is the devil and demons there right now as their headquarters? No, but may be cast there in the future depending on your eschatology.

Myth #5
There is nothing that God cannot do.

At one time or another, we have all heard, *With God all things are possible. (Matt. 19:26)* so there is nothing that God cannot do, right? There are many who respond with these words without really thinking them through, and it's often just a phrase we throw out there when we don't know what else to say like, "God is in control" (future myth). The truth is that it is a myth. There are many things that God cannot do and not because of a lack of ability, but He limits Himself to His word and character. So here are just a few things God cannot do so you can share them:

1. God cannot fail (I Cor. 13) Love never fails: He is love
2. God cannot lie (Heb. 6:18)
3. God cannot stop loving you (Jer. 31:3 & I John 4:19)
4. God cannot sleep (Ps. 121:4)
5. God cannot get tired (Isaiah 40:28)
6. God cannot change (Mal. 3:6 & Heb. 13:8)
7. God cannot be fooled (Num. 32:23)
8. God cannot forget you (Isaiah 49:15)
9. God cannot be divided (John 10:30)
10. God cannot remember your sins (Heb. 8:12)

There are more things God cannot do, but these are just a few of my favorites, so when you hear someone say these quotes, do not rebuke them, just kindly mention that it isn't true and then share some of these. It's also a neat study to do.

Myth #6
God is in control.

When we hear the phrase, 'God is in control' it is normally something we say when things happen that we are unsure about and we don't know what else to say. An example would be when someone we know is going through a divorce or when someone is diagnosed with a sickness and we say, "God is in control". Now if we would think that through, we would realize that God is not the author of sickness and He had nothing to do with that marriage falling apart. We don't know what else to say, so we fall back on the 'God is in control' card. God is sovereign, which means He is King and supreme and this Earth is the Lords and all that is within it, but He is NOT in control of everything that happens on it. I own a 200 x 200 lot, it's mine. I am the king of that property, but I can't control what the squirrels or the skunks (that like to get under my back deck) or everything my kids do on that property.

God says in Genesis 1:26, *Let Us make man in Our image, according to Our likeness, and let THEM rule over the fish of the sea and the birds of the sky and over the cattle and over all the earth, and over every creeping thing that creeps on the earth.* Notice, God did not say, "Let Us make them and let Us have dominion" but instead, He gave the authority of the Earth realm to mankind. Psalms

115:16; *The Heavens are the heavens of the Lord, but the Earth He has given to the sons of men.* When Adam rebelled, it caused the curse and all this mess that has happened on the Earth. It also opened the door to sin and death and gave the devil the right to wreak havoc on mankind and fill it with fear rather than faith; hate rather than love; and war rather than peace.

If everything that happens on the Earth is God controlling it like a puppet master, then we would have to believe that He is in control of ISIS, the sex slave trade, rape, disease, and all war and violence; and if He did everything He gets blamed for, then not one nation on the planet would allow Him in their borders. We know that these issues are men with unregenerate minds, who are doing horrible things that God has NOTHING to do with.

When we say, 'God is in control' we may not be thinking this way, but when others hear us say things like that their reaction is, "If God is in control of all this, then I don't want anything to do with Him" and who can blame them? The Good News however, is that God started over with the last Adam, Jesus Christ, and He came to reconcile and turn everything right side up again through a new creation.

When we allow His love to work through us, then we are called as the sons of God, to put this creation right again. This is why Paul said in

Romans 8, *All creation is groaning for the manifestation of the sons of God."* God gave mankind the control of this Earth and He now lives His life in and thru the sons of the Kingdom, to turn this graveyard of an Earth back into a garden once again. So, realize that we are co-laborers with Christ and without Him, we can do nothing but without us, He won't.

Myth #7
The devil is omnipresent.

There's a misunderstanding in many sincere and well-meaning people about the devil and his abilities. For years, as I have traveled around the globe, I have had people ask me to pray for them and many have started by saying, "The devil has really been attacking my family, finances, physical body, etc." Now I'm always gracious, but I also say to them that it is highly unlikely that THE devil, himself, has been coming after them and their family, since he can only be in one place at one time. Most of their issues come from wrong decisions, wrong thinking, disobedience, believing lies, or a demonic spirit that has attached itself to them or their family, but not the actual devil.

The devil is not God; neither is he Gods equal counterpart. Now Santa may see you when you're sleeping and know when you're awake lol, but satan does not. We have given way too much authority to a defeated devil, and at times we put him on par with God. I highly doubt that most believers are doing so much harm against the kingdom of darkness or been given so much revelation that it would cause the devil himself to show up and deal with them. The Scriptures tell us that the adversary, the devil, goes about as a roaring lion seeking whom he may devour; notice, not who he CAN devour, but who he MAY devour. According to Job, he walks and roams the Earth, if he was omnipresent he would already be there. In other words, he must have permission and an open door; and he can only be at one place at a time, just like Michael the archangel is not everywhere present, only God is. Are the devil and demons real? Perhaps, but not all powerful, or all knowing, or omnipresent, and we all need to realize that we do have enemies who are out to hinder us and keep us from experiencing the freedom of the Kingdom. However, to most, our greatest enemy is ourselves, as Commodore Oliver Perry said in a now famous quote; "We have met our enemy, and our enemy is us.

Myth #8
The world is going to end.

Most of us have heard at one time or another about end of the World scenarios. Some of it was in the movies, the Sci-fi channel or our very own end time T.V. preachers or pastors, as well as books and myths from many major ancient religions. Those of us who are Christians have also heard this from the time we were young, and they probably got us running to the altar a few times to get saved again, lol. What do the Scriptures actually say about an ending to this World or this Earth? Would it surprise you to find out it says absolutely nothing, nada, zippo, nothing at all about it. Unless you read some translations, who did a poor job of translating the Greek word 'aion' (age) or a literal reading of 2 Peter 3, which still ends in unrighteousness being removed and the Earth cleansed, but not coming to an end. It mainly comes from the disciples asking Jesus in Matthew 24:3, *What will be the sign of your coming and the end of the 'World'?* (KJV). The word 'World' in most other translations is age, because it is the Greek word 'aion' (an age, epoch, a cycle or a season and sometimes depending on the context, eternity). It was also translated as 'World' incorrectly in Matthew 13:39 & 49; *and the enemy who sowed them is the devil, and the harvest is the end of the age; and the reapers are angels. So, it will be at the end of the age; the angels will come forth and take out the wicked from among the righteous.*

However, Paul tells us in Eph. 3:21, *Unto Him be glory in the church by Christ Jesus, through-out all ages, World without end, Amen* (or an age without end). We are also told in Ecc.1:4, *The Earth remains forever* and in Psalms 78:69, *And He built His sanctuary like the heights, like the earth which He has founded forever*, and Psalm 93:1, *The LORD reigns, He is clothed with majesty; The LORD has clothed and girded Himself with strength; Indeed, the world is firmly established, it will not be moved*; and Psalm 96:10, *Say among the nations, The LORD reigns; Indeed, the world is firmly established, it will not be moved, He will judge the peoples with equity.* This tells us, all three times, that the World is firmly forever established, and it will not be moved. Also, in Isaiah 45:1, *You shall not be ashamed or confounded, 'World' without end.* 'World' in Hebrew is 'Olam' (long duration, eternity, forever, ages) so God has continually said that this Earth and 'World' are never going to come to an end but will be transformed. The Jews call it 'Tikkun Olam' (a repairing and renovation of the World).

My friends just know that all of us, one day, will have this 'World' end 'to us' (but it will not end). So, do not live in fear of the end of the 'World' and let's get busy advancing the Father's renovation project that was started at the cross in Christ Jesus' death and Resurrection.

Myth #9
The righteous/church will leave planet earth.

Many have been taught either through authors and movies such as 'Left behind' that the righteous/church will be evacuated someday and leave planet Earth for either three and a half or seven years, depending on what pre-millennial teacher you listen to. Much of our futuristic end time teachings seem to hope and pray that the other team finally wins so we can all leave the field. I mean, if we really believe it has to get worse and the sky has to be falling for Jesus to come, then why do so many Christians freak out about politics, gay marriage, ISIS, etc. I believe it is because the Holy Spirit on the inside of us is stirring us to change the world, but much of our teachings have caused us to believe it has to get worse and it doesn't matter what we do, which has led to much fear and confusion. I have put the challenge out on Facebook several times, as well as asked many 'end time' experts to prove me wrong by giving the Scriptures that prove otherwise and no one has been successful.

Now I believe that Jesus is going to return physically at 'The Resurrection' in the future (yes, I am still Orthodox enough to embrace this, lol) but I do not believe that the Church will leave for Heaven, but Heaven is coming to Earth. He is returning with 10,000's of His saints, and what has been called the 'Blessed hope' is 'THE Resurrection and our receiving a glorified body'. The main reason why I call this a myth is because there are no Scriptures that clearly show this, and the one normally used is found in 1 Thess.4:17 and even that one tells us we will be caught up (Harpazo- to seize, to snatch, caught up) but not leave. Now to build any doctrine or belief system, it is wise for it to be established in the mouth of '2 or 3 witness' which proper hermeneutics (the study of interpretation) tells us, and you normally do not build a belief system on a single verse. There are no other clear Scriptures that speak of the righteous/church leaving the planet period. However, there are at least 15 that show us the righteous/church will never leave. Plus, I believe that if Jesus prayed in John 17:15, *My prayer is that you NOT take them out of this World*, then that is what the heart of the Father is also. Many in the church have been praying to leave and Jesus prayed that we would stay, so whose prayers do we think are going to be answered?

Some also use the story of Noah as an example but in that story, it was the wicked that left and the righteous that stayed, just like in the parable of the wheat and the tares in Matthew 13:36-43, the tares were removed, and the wheat stayed. We are also told in Proverbs 10:30, *The righteous shall never be removed and the wicked shall not inherit the Earth*. Psalms 2:8, Psalms

37:9,11, 22, 29,34; Psalms 89:36 as well as Proverbs 2:21, 22; Proverbs 10:25, Proverbs 12:3,7 and Matthew 5:5 also share similar ideas. There is overwhelming Scriptural evidence of the righteous inheriting planet Earth as well as Jesus telling us the meek would also, and there are no Scriptures that prove otherwise.

Now, whatever you choose to embrace as your end time view, just know that anything other than what historically has already taken place is just 'theory' period, because none of us know for sure. I also want to encourage you to study it out for yourself and if I am wrong, then prove me wrong and I will repent and retract, but please don't believe something just because you were taught it by someone you love. So, I'm calling the evacuation plan cancelled and pure myth, for Jesus is not the Savior FROM the World, but the Savior OF the World. Instead, let us all occupy (do business) till He comes, and participate with the help of the Holy Spirit in the Fathers renovation plan that was started at the cross in Christ Jesus.

Myth #10
Faith comes by the Bible/Scriptures.

The apostle Paul tells us in Romans 10:17, *Now faith comes by hearing and hearing by the word of God/Christ.* The older translations say 'word of God' but the newer ones say 'Christ' which is correct from the original Greek. In other words, it is the good news of Christ (anointed one, messiah) that produces faith (trust, belief confidence) in us. There are many things written in the Scriptures that do not produce faith in us and are not written 'to' us but are there 'for' us to learn from. The problem is, we hear leaders say quite often, "Every promise in the book is mine." without really thinking it through. There are a lot of promises that have already been fulfilled and a lot of them, you don't want. Whenever we reduce the Scriptures down to a book of blessings and promises, it causes us to forget that it is also full of death, judgements, wrath, and warnings that were also promises. We must always remember that when we read, study, and interpret, we do it through the lens of Jesus and the New Covenant or it can get us into all kinds of crazy beliefs.

We are told by Paul in Romans 15:4, *For whatever was written in earlier times was written for our instruction, so that through perseverance and the encouragement of the Scriptures we might have hope.* The Scriptures testify of Jesus; the law and the prophets spoke of Him, and the sum of the book speaks of Him. However, Paul also told us in 2 Corinthians 3:6, *The letter kills, but the Spirit gives life.* Also, in Galatians 3:23, *But before faith came, we were kept in custody under the law, being shut up to the faith which was later to be revealed.* Jesus also told the Pharisees in John 5:39, *You study the Scriptures because you think that in them you have eternal life; it is these that testify of me.* So, both Paul and Jesus made it pretty clear that the Scriptures can 'shut up faith' 'the letter can kill', and 'eternal life' is NOT found in them. This does not diminish the need or importance of the Scriptures because God moved upon and inspired men to write them and they are there for teaching, correction, reproof, and instruction, but they do not all produce faith.

There are many things we read like Lamentations that normally do not inspire a lot of trust and confidence, or the 'Begat's' lol. I could quote Deut. 22:20-21 that says, *If a woman is found on her wedding night to not be a virgin, she should be taken out and stoned.* Well, that is not going to produce any faith (trust, belief, and confidence) in any women who is not a virgin, but it is in the Bible. So just know that it is the Gospel of Christ and the hearing of the Good News of the Kingdom that produces faith in those who will hear and believe.

Myth #11
Jesus talked about Hell more than Heaven and any other topic.

Many of us have heard the above statement in some form or another through the years, and many well-known leaders, teacher and authors have boldly taught and said it. Now, let me start by saying that there is a place translated as hell in the Scriptures that is real (hades-grave, Gehenna-valley of Hinnom) so this myth is NOT about differing views on hell or who will or will not be there (that is up to God to judge). I am simply wanting to de-bunk the myth that Jesus talked more about it than anything else, which is NOT true. Depending on what translation you use, and I use the NASB, the word 'hell' is found 15 times in the whole bible and 11 times in the Gospels. Jesus refers to it along with several other Scriptures that reverence judgment and punishment.

Also, in the Septuagint Bible (Greek rendering of the whole Bible) along with several literal translations such as the YLT, you will not even find the word 'hell' at all. Instead, it is translated as 'grave, pit, depths, or Gehenna' (an actual valley outside of Jerusalem). It is also translated once as 'Tartarus' which was the Greek prison for the Titans in Greek Mythology, found only in II Peter and was one of the reasons II Peter was one of the most argued books to be allowed in the Canon.

The actual name 'hell' comes from an old German word, 'hel' which means to cover or veil, which was not even introduced until the 8th century or so and before that, it was simply 'grave, pit and Gehenna' (Valley of Hinnom) a place known to the Jews as a place of death, burning, judgment and garbage. In the Sermon on the Mount alone, Jesus talks about 'The Kingdom of Heaven' 11 times. As a matter of fact, there are 123 references to the Kingdom of Heaven' in the New Testament and a majority of them are used by Jesus. More than 190 verses are Jesus speaking about the Kingdom of Heaven, eternal life, or the Kingdom of God which is the same as the Kingdom of Heaven, so there is NOTHING HE talked about more than the Kingdom and how to live and function it.

In the Book of Acts, there are 17 or more sermons preached and not one of them deal with the after-life, heaven or hell. Their message was about a new King with a new government, faith towards God, repenting of religion and sin, a self-sacrificing love, a fresh start, completely forgiven of their sin and the past. That does not diminish the reality of heaven, hell or the idea that they should be taught or not; but it was just not the focus of the apostle's message. Their message was how to live in the nasty now and not how to get to the sweet by and by, lol.

It has been mainly in the last 500 years or so that the message has become more about the afterlife rather than the present reality of the King and His Kingdom. So, rather than focus on getting to heaven and escaping hell, why don't we focus instead on bringing Heaven to Earth which by the way will produce both of those. AS my good friend, Dr. Lynn Hiles says, "Rather than just focusing on making Heaven my home, I want to make my home more like Heaven."

Myth #12
The 'thief' who steals, kills and destroys is the devil.

The passage in John 10:10, *The thief comes to steal, kill and destroy, but I have come that you might have life and have it to the full.* Is not referring to the devil, but the law and false shepherds that come any other way than through the door to get the sheep. When you study the whole passage starting at the end of John 9 and follow through to 10:1-12, Jesus is speaking to the Scribes and Pharisees and boldly telling them that they are wolves, false shepherds, thieves and robbers. He tells them in Matt. 21:13, *My house shall be called a house of prayer, but you have turned it into a den of robbers and thieves.* Also, in Matt. 23:14, *Woe to you Scribes and Pharisees, hypocrites; for you devour widow's houses.*

Jesus also called them white washed tombs or places of death and not life. Then in Matt. 7:15, *Watch out for false prophets for they come to you in sheep's clothing, but inside are ravenous wolves.* Jesus is letting the religious system know that they are not true shepherds, as they have titles and are self-appointed. To them, it is just a job which is why Jesus also calls them 'hirelings' which are those who scatter the sheep because they do not have the heart of the Good Shepherd.

Now is the fruit of the devil to steal, kill and destroy? Sure. Could this also be a metaphor to describe the character of the enemy of our souls? Perhaps. He does those things, but in the context and in proper interpretation of Scripture, we must first ask; "Who was the original audience and what did it mean to them and then, how is this applicable to us?" Jesus in this passage was speaking about the priests and the false shepherds of that day and letting everyone know that they were putting people into bondage with the law, but He was releasing them into life and freedom by the law of liberty. Jesus is light, life, and love according to 'I John' and there is no darkness, death, or fear in Him, period.

Myth #13
God and evil cannot be in the same place.

A good portion of us have probably heard the above statement, at one time or another, just like Myth #3, (God cannot look on sin) which is NOT true. The above idea comes from the understanding that God is light and there is no darkness IN Him which is true, but it can be and is around Him. In the book of Job 1:6 Satan is standing in the throne room, with the sons of God, talking to God; *Now there was a day when the sons of God came to present themselves before the LORD, and Satan also came among them.* So evil, himself, was in God's presence in His own house. David, in Psalms 23:4, tells us, *Even though I walk through the valley of the shadow of death, I fear no evil, for You are with me; Your rod and Your staff, they comfort me.* Right there in the presence of evil is God with us. Also, Romans 7:21, *So I find this law at work; although I want to do good, evil is right there with me.* So, Paul is telling us that evil is present at the same time as good along with God's love and presence.

If God and evil cannot be in the same vicinity than there would be no evil because God is omniscient and everywhere all at once, and Paul tells us that He is above all, through all, and in all, and Jeremiah 23 says He fills Heaven and Earth. In 2 Chronicles 18:20, a lying spirit came into the throne room of Heaven and has a conversation with God about Ahab, Vs. 18-20, *Micaiah said, 'Therefore, hear the word of the LORD. I saw the LORD sitting on His throne, and all the host of heaven standing on His right and on His left. The LORD said, 'Who will entice Ahab king of Israel to go up and fall at Ramoth-gilead?' And one said this while another said that. Then a spirit came forward and stood before the LORD and said, 'I will entice him.'* And we know that God hates lying and all sin and yet there it is in His presence. David also tells us in Psalm 139:7-8, *Where can I go from your presence, if I ascend to Heaven you are there; and if I make my bed in hell (sheol or grave) behold, you are there.* I'm not sure there is a place which is more evil than that and yet, He is even there.

So just know my friends that there is no place that God is not, for if there is, then that thing or place has become God in itself and must sustain itself. He is above all, through all, in all, and fills all things. God hates sin and evil because of what it does to His creation, but it is not kryptonite to Him nor does it weaken Him; not only that, but where sin and evil abound that is a good candidate for grace to abound even more.

Myth #14
Some demons are only cast out by prayer and fasting.

This is a mistranslation that was added by most of the translators of the older versions of the Bible but is left out of most of the newer ones because it is not in the Greek text. It comes from Mark 9:29, *This kind only comes out by prayer and fasting.* (KJV & NKJV) but just prayer in most of the newer translations; fasting is not there in the ESV or the NASB which are widely regarded as two of the most. literal, with the Greek text.

Jesus gave the disciples authority over demon spirits, but they were struggling in their attempt to cast this one out. Jesus then walked up and dealt with it easily. The disciples ask Him, "Why couldn't we?" When we study the whole context the point of the story is not just about prayer and fasting or the casting out of a demon, but 'unbelief'. Jesus shows up and He says in V19, *How long shall I put up with you 'unbelieving' generation?* and then says in Vs.23, *All things are possible to him who believes.* So, the message of the story is, the disciples were struggling with 'unbelief' and not necessarily a more powerful demon.

They had been given authority over the power of the enemy and this kind is dealt with through prayer that removes unbelief. In other words, prayer builds our faith and removes unbelief, so we can manifest with greater confidence the authority He has given us. Maybe that is why we are told to, "Pray in the Spirit, building up our most holy faith". However, fasting is NOT a bad thing at all and a great discipline, but it is not needed to cast out a demon, we need only believe in the authority Christ has freely given to us to do that.

Myth #15
The truth will set you free!

This statement is a true statement and it is in the Bible, but it is only part of a verse and cannot be taken out of context to mean something different than what it actually says. John 8:31&32, *If you continue in my Word, then you are truly disciples of mine, and you will know the truth and the truth will set you free.* So, it is NOT just the truth that sets us free, but the truth that we 'know' (come to know by first-hand experience). Also, that which has become realized. Many hear truth and it is true and freeing, but only when it is experienced and applied does it actually set us free.

Paul told Timothy there would be some who are *'always learning' but never coming to the knowledge of the truth* (2 Timothy 3:7). This also applies to those who are hearers of the Word and not doers of the Word. Jesus says that they build their house on the sand and not the rock. Ignorance is not bliss, and what we do not know can hurt us, *My people are destroyed for a lack of knowledge* (Hosea 4:6). Yet, it is in walking out the truth we have learned, in our everyday lives, that sets us free; not just getting in a prayer line, getting a prophecy at a conference or in reading a book about freedom. Those things are all good, but if we do not act on them, then there will be no 'fruit of the truth' that brings freedom. Maybe this is why Jesus washed the disciple's feet (walk) because that is what He was most concerned with.

Myth #16
Saying OMG is taking the name of the Lord in vain.

When I was a kid I got my mouth washed out with soap for saying 'gosh' because it was slang for God; and then once for saying 'Jeez' because that was slang for Jesus; saying that was taking the name of the Lord in vain. What never clicked was how is 'saying something 'taking' something in vain? It always bothered me and it never made sense as 'God is NOT His name, but a description of all earthly deities. IN the Old Testament, God's name was not pronounceable since they had no vowels. The closet was Yahweh and Jehovah minus the vowels, so try to pronounce or say that. Lol

Exodus 20:7, *You shall not take the name of the Lord your God in vain.* This is one of the big ten, but what does it mean? Do we believe that saying God Da****t, or OMG is breaking this commandment, or did it mean something different to the Hebrews and the Jews, the ones who it was written to? I asked a Messianic Rabbi, several years ago, what that commandment meant and he laughed and said, "Probably nothing like your American Western Christian church has taught you.

The word 'take' means, to lift, carry, bring forth, accept, and take, so to accept and to carry the name of the Lord in vain changes the whole idea.

The Rabbi explained that when my wife married me she took or accepted my name, and for her to do that in vain (falsehood, deceit, emptiness, and lies) would be if she then left me and ran off with another man and divorced me the next week.

To 'take' the name of the Lord in vain is to call yourself His and then have little or no desire to live like you are His or have a relationship with Him. It also gives an inference to anyone who proclaims His name falsely as in 'thus says the Lord' or 'God told me' when He did not. It has more to do with our living and representing God properly in our lifestyles than it does just our verbiage.

So, it's NOT by saying OMG that we break this commandment (which we are no longer under by the way, since the law was never given to Gentiles, but to the Jews) or 'Oh Lord, or G*d D***.' However, if doing that is a stumbling block to others, then we should not according to Romans 14:13, *Therefore, let us not judge one another anymore, but rather determine this...not to put an obstacle or a stumbling block in a brother's way.* Also, please do not correct people for it, especially unbelievers, since it is not what it means anyway.

Myth #17
The blessing of Malachi 3 is from giving ten percent of your income.

If you have been in a church service at any time in your life, you have probably heard quoted around the offering time Malachi 3:8-10, *Will a man rob God? Yet you are robbing me! But you say, 'How have we robbed you?' 'In tithes and offerings. You are cursed with a curse, for you are robbing me, the whole nation of you. Bring all the tithes (the whole tithe) into the storehouse so that there may be meat in my house, and test me now in this, says the Lord of hosts, if I will not open for you the windows of Heaven and pour you out a blessing that you cannot contain.'* Many of us were then taught, in some form, that this was speaking of giving 10 percent of our income to the Church or our storehouse, and if we did this it would open Heaven to us and reverse the curse.

The problem with that is that 10 percent is NOT what Malachi 3 is speaking about but is actually referring to between 20-30 percent which represented ALL the tithe(S). Somehow in teaching this, many left out the plurality of tithes and offerings of which this refers to in the Old Testament. The Hebrews were instructed to give first-fruits; Terumah' (also referred to as 'heave offerings') to the high priest; along with tithes and offerings that totaled more than 23 percent at least;

depending on what scholar you read. They were instructed to give at least three tithes, one was 10 percent, to the Levites Lev 27:30-32, *Thus all the tithe of the land, of the seed of the land or of the fruit of the tree, is the LORD'S; it is holy to the LORD. If, therefore, a man wishes to redeem part of his tithe, he shall add to it one-fifth of it. For every tenth part of herd or flock, whatever passes under the rod, the tenth one shall be holy to the LORD.* Another was to themselves, so they could travel to Jerusalem to celebrate the feasts, Deut. 14:22-27, *You shall surely tithe all the produce from what you sow, which comes out of the field every year. You shall eat in the presence of the LORD your God, at the place where He chooses to establish His name, the tithe of your grain, your new wine, your oil, and the firstborn of your herd and your flock, so that you may learn to fear the LORD your God always. If the distance is so great for you that you are not able to bring the tithe, since the place where the LORD your God chooses to set His name is too far away from you when the LORD your God blesses you, then you shall exchange it for money, and bind the money in your hand and go to the place which the LORD your God chooses. You may spend the money for whatever your heart desires: for oxen, or sheep, or wine, or strong drink, or whatever your heart desires; and there you shall eat in the presence of the LORD your God and rejoice, you and your household. Also, you shall not neglect the Levite who is in your town, for he has no portion or inheritance among you*

Then once every 3 years, they were to give one tenth to the poor Deut. *14:28-29, At the end of every third year, you shall bring out all the tithe of your produce in that year and shall deposit it in your town. The Levite, because he has no portion or inheritance among you, and the alien, the orphan and the widow who are in your town, shall come and eat and be satisfied, in order that the LORD your God may bless you in all the work of your hand which you do.*

Then you have different offerings; temple taxes etc. So, giving 10 percent does not even come close to activating the Malachi 3 blessing or removing the curse. My point to this myth is to simply show that giving 10 percent does not fulfill Malachi 3 period. I am not trying to, nor will discuss whether tithing is for today because that is NOT the point of this myth, and you can all study that for yourselves.

Myth #18
The power of God and the gifts of the Spirit only manifest in your life after the in-filling of the Holy Spirit.

I grew up in the Pentecostal/Charismatic world where this was taught quite a bit and inferred at other times. I had a class in Bible college called, 'Pentecostal Distinctive's' which was all about what made us unique or distinct from the rest of the body of Christ. My first statement after the 3rd class was, "Isn't this what divides us from the rest?" It was then taught that if the disciples needed to be endued with power, so do we (which I still believe by the way) and until then, we are saved but pretty much powerless, which is not true. I still remember sermons saying, "You need to get the Holy Spirit" when the truth was, we needed to yield to the Holy Spirit in us and let Him get us. The problem with this mindset is that the disciples were raising the dead, healing the sick, and casting out demons before they ever spoke in tongues at Pentecost. Jesus gave them power (Greek; exousia; power, authority might) over sickness, disease and the enemy) and this is given to every believer who has the name of Jesus and the Spirit of Christ living in them.

This is why our non-Pentecostal friends could heal the sick and cast out devils and we didn't know what to do with that. However, what changed at Pentecost was, they were given a new language which they did not have before and they started working together and stopped fighting. What Pentecost brought was unity (one accord) between the brothers, as well as an added stick of dynamite (dunamis power and might) to the exousia they already had. So, is the infilling and overflowing of the Holy Spirit a good thing in our lives? Absolutely, but it does not manifest the gifts and the power of the Holy Spirit; these are given at salvation and then manifested by faith (1 Cor. 14).

    The in-filling of the Holy Spirit is an explosion and an awareness of what we already have in Christ, which is why Jesus said, "Out of your belly shall flow rivers of living water" and not a deluge dropping down on you from the sky; Ephesians 1:3, *You have BEEN blessed with EVERY spiritual blessing in the Heavenly Christ.* He has placed within us all things that pertain to life and Godliness, we just need an awareness and an explosion out of us which is what the 'baptism' of the Spirit is, and it is a gift by faith that we do not have to beg or 'tarry' for.

Myth #19
The 'sinner's prayer' and 'altar calls' are how people have always come to Christ.

I am a preacher's kid and grew up in Church. I remember how rare it was if we didn't end the service with an altar call for salvation and then lead people in what is known as 'The sinner's prayer' of which I prayed a hundred times, lol. Now I'm not saying it's a bad thing or something we shouldn't do, especially since our culture is used to it and Romans 10:10 tells us, *confession is made unto salvation*. What I am doing is unraveling the myth of 'This is how it has always been done.'

There is not one example in the book of Acts, when the Gospel was being preached and someone was converted, that they were told to do anything other than believe, repent, and be baptized. Throughout church history there is rarely a time altar calls were done, until the great reformation, and even then, there were only a few who taught this. It wasn't until the 1800's, under evangelist Charles Finney, it became a theology; it was then made popular by evangelist Billy Sunday in the 20th century, especially in the U.S. Billy would have people walk down front to shake his hand.

The famous 19th century preacher, John Wesley, would end his sermons with "Believe on the Lord and you will be saved". He was asked, after preaching to a large audience, "How do you know if anyone was converted"? He responded by saying, "When I come back in 6-9 months and they are in a local church and bearing fruit, then I will tell them that they are saved." This of course would not be impressive in a monthly newsletter or a Facebook post about how many 'got saved' on Sunday, lol. I had once participated with a street evangelism team that came into our area in the late 90's. They gave us a script to take with us on the streets to lead people to Christ. We prayed in a park with one man and it was so easy that I wanted to talk with him more. He admitted to me that he had prayed the prayer at least 15 times with people because he figured out they would leave him alone if he did that. They had reported that more than 30,000 people had received Christ over several months of them being there.

Now, I have no doubt that some had genuine experiences, but Jesus did NOT tell us to go and get people 'saved' but to go and make disciples. So, my friends, whether a leader does this or not is not the point, but we should not believe that this is THE way it is done but can be 'A' way. Just make sure that we go on and make disciples and win souls (mind, will, emotions) and not just have someone repeat a prayer without our care or follow up.

Myth #20
Jesus was crucified on Good Friday.

Let me start by saying that 'when' we celebrate and honor something should not be the point, but the fact that we 'do' honor and celebrate it. We celebrate Christmas as the birth of Jesus and yet, He was not born near December at all; the point is that we celebrate His arrival as a gift to us every year. We celebrate the death, burial, and resurrection of Jesus between Good Friday and Sunday a.m., but in our hearts, we celebrate it every day and that is the message we live and proclaim. However, trying to fit 3 days and 3 nights into Friday thru Sunday a.m. can only be done with common core math, lol.

In Matthew 12, Jesus says that a wicked generation seeks after a sign and THE only sign given is that the Son of Man would be like Jonah in the belly of the fish for three days and three nights in the heart of the Earth. Now, to a Jew, their days were and still are from sundown to sundown because in Genesis, God separated the days from the evening till the morning. Some theologians then say that because of that, it was three days from Friday afternoon (one day) then Saturday (second day) then Sunday (third day) but the problem is that Jesus said, 'three days and three nights.'

Many others argue that Jesus was crucified on Wednesday before dark, then they prepared His body before the Sabbath, which because it was Passover, this was referring to one of the 'high' Sabbaths which was Wednesday (sundown) to Thursday (sundown) and not the regular Saturday one. John 19:31 tells us that it was the preparation day before the Sabbath and it was a High Day Sabbath which Leviticus 23 called one of the seven 'Annual' Sabbaths. The prisoners had to then be taken down before the Sabbath to be prepared for burial, which is why many believe that it was Friday as that was the normal preparation day.

However, Passover week is different, and we also have Matthew 28:1, *the women went to the tomb after the Sabbath towards the first day of the week.* This is a mistranslation because in the Greek, it is Sabbath's (plural). In Mark's gospel, it says the women bought the spices after the Sabbath, which they were unable to do on the Sabbath since nothing was open and they were not allowed.

Then, in Luke's gospel it says, *They prepared the spices and oils before resting on the Sabbath.* So there had to be two different Sabbaths to even make sense of it all. With this timeline it allows for three days and nights. Wednesday p.m. to Thursday p.m. (1) Thursday p.m. to Friday p.m. (2) and Friday p.m. to Saturday p.m. (3). He rose on the 3rd day, while it was still dark, then Mary discovered the tomb in the a.m. on the first day of the week.

Both theories are interesting, and which one is right will probably be argued until Jesus returns lol, but I do know that you can NOT fit in three days and nights between Friday p.m. and Sunday a.m. period, which was the point of this myth.

Myth #21
There are many races of people on the earth.

There is not one Scripture that refers to human beings as being any other race than the **Human Race**, period. Yet, there are Scriptures that tell us that we all come from 'one blood' Acts17:26, And *he made from one every nation of men to live on all the face of the earth, having determined allotted periods and the boundaries of their habitation;* as well as Gal 3:28, *There is neither Jew nor Greek, there is neither slave nor free, there is neither male nor female;* **for you are all one in Christ Jesus.**

I like to tease people by saying, "Adam (red, ruddy) came from dirt, which has color and is dark, but Eve came from bone which is pale; whitish and gray. So, we all come from a daddy who was a man of color and a white momma" (which may explain where we got all these colors from, lol). We are all made in the image and likeness of God, Gen 1:26-27, *Then God said, Let Us make man in Our image, according to Our likeness; and let them rule over the fish of the sea and over the birds of the-sky and over the cattle and over all the earth, and over every creeping thing that creeps on the earth. God created man in His own image, in the image of God He created him; male and female He created them.* and James 3:9 tells us the same thing, *with it we bless our Lord and Father, and with it we curse men, who have been made in the likeness of God.*

Now there are different cultures, tongues, tribes, peoples, and nations according to Rev 7:9-10, *After this I looked, and behold, a great multitude which no man could number, from every nation, from all tribes and peoples and tongues, standing before the throne and before the Lamb, clothed in white robes, with palm branches in their hands, and crying out with a loud voice, "Salvation belongs to our God who sits upon the throne, and to the Lamb."* God does not have a race card. When you put two animals together you get an animal, two humans together you get a human, period. The Heavenly Father see's humans on the planet as His Offspring Acts 17, *and that He is the Father of every family named in Heaven and Earth.* Eph. 3:15, *from whom every family in heaven and on earth is named.*

When we put people into racial categories, it allows demonizing and prejudice to be prevalent. If I can convince people that 'one race' of people are inferior to another, then they can scapegoat them and not feel bad about demeaning, enslaving, or killing them. The Jews had this mentality with Gentiles, and to them, loving your neighbor as yourself was loving other Jews and not Gentiles. This is why they tried to kill Jesus a few times, because He said God loves Samaritans and Gentiles and they should also.

Slave owners in the U.S. were taught by their pastors, who owned slaves, that black people did not have souls. Hitler convinced a generation of young Germans, raised in the Lutheran church for the most part, that Jews were Christ killers and deserved to be exterminated. This was not a stretch, because Martin Luther was extremely anti-Semitic. Any time we put a focus on 'race' it will cause one to feel superior to another. So please, can we change our verbiage in the church and rather than say we have a multi-racial church, can we just call it multi-cultural? Also, can we please stop saying there are 'mixed' race children, which only serves to cause them, at times, to think they don't fit anywhere. ALL of us are different shades of dirt, but ultimately, we are ALL just dirt and we will return to dirt someday. So, let's celebrate our uniqueness and not let them divide us but unite us in understanding that to know our Heavenly Father, we need to see the 'full' expression of His image and likeness on the Earth, which is the whole Human race which is beautiful.

Myth #22
There was no room for Jesus and His family in the Inn (motel).

In the late 90's I preached a Christmas message at my parent's church. I brought out the mistranslation that has turned into a myth of Christian tradition; that Mary and Joseph had to stay in a stable to give birth to Jesus, because there was no vacancy at the Bethlehem Inn. Luke 2:7, *And she gave birth to her firstborn son; and she wrapped Him in cloths, and laid Him in a manger, because there was no room for them in the inn.*

First of all, the word translated as 'inn' (Kataluma) means 'guest chamber' and is used by Luke to also describe the room where Jesus had the last supper with His disciples. When Luke is talking about a motel or an actual inn, he uses the word (pandeion) which describes where the good Samaritan had taken the man who had been robbed. Most newer translations correctly interpret this by saying guest room or guest chamber.

We must also understand that Mary and Joseph were going back to his hometown where his family was from, and he was from the line of King David, so he no doubt would have not only stayed with family, but others in the town would have took them in, especially as a descendant of David. Plus, according to Deut. 10:19, *So show your love for the alien, for you were aliens in the land of Egypt.* The Hebrews were instructed to love and take in strangers, and to this day in the middle East they would not turn a stranger away, especially one about to give birth.

We don't know the exact circumstances, but they could have had other family already in the guest chamber, so they would have stayed downstairs in the foyer area; a step lower than the living room, where they had built in feeding troughs, and where the families would bring many of their animals in at night for protection and warmth. Another scenario is; because she was pregnant and not married, under the law, she could have been stoned and the family could have been struggling with that fact and not let them use the guest chamber.

The truth is, we really don't know what happened, the Scriptures do not make it clear. However, the pictures of baby Jesus, the shepherds and the three wise men or kings along with the animals in a barn look nice in our yards and in front of churches at Christmas time, but did not happen that way.

Myth #23
There will be a 'final' judgment day.

In many of our Bibles, there are headings above chapters and certain passages; several translations put the words 'final judgement' above those passages. These are of course added by man as the words 'final judgement' are NOT found anywhere in the Scriptures. Matthew 25:31-46 is one example of this, as well as Revelation 20:11-14. These have written above them 'the final judgement' with bold print in many translations. Now, will there be 'A judgement day' according to Scripture? I believe so, and it is for all of humanity, for the quick and the dead 1Peter 4:5-7, *but they will give account to Him who is ready to judge the living and the dead. For the gospel has for this purpose been preached even to those who are dead, that though they are judged in the flesh as men, they may live in the spirit according to the will of God. The end of all things is near; therefore, be of sound judgment and sober spirit for the purpose of prayers.*

II Timothy 4, *I solemnly charge you in the presence of God and of Christ Jesus, who is to judge the living and the dead, and by His appearing and His kingdom.* and the just and the unjust all will be raised and stand before Him after the Resurrection. Acts, 24:15, *Having a hope in God, which these men cherish themselves, that there shall certainly be a resurrection of both the righteous and the wicked.* Matt. 25:31-46 *But when the Son of Man comes in His glory, and all the angels with Him, then He will sit on His glorious throne. All the nations will be gathered before Him; and He will separate them from one another, as the shepherd separates the sheep from the goats; and He will put the sheep on His right, and the goats on the left. Then the King will say to those on His right, 'Come, you who are blessed of My Father, inherit the kingdom prepared for you from the foundation of the world. For I was hungry, and you gave Me something to eat; I was thirsty, and you gave Me something to drink; I was a stranger, and you invited Me in; naked, and you clothed Me; I was sick, and you visited Me; I was in prison, and you came to Me.' Then the righteous will answer Him, 'Lord, when did we see You hungry, and feed You, or thirsty, and give You something to drink? And when did we see You a stranger, and invite You in, or naked, and clothe You? When did we see You sick, or in prison, and come to You?' The King will answer and say to them, 'Truly I say to you, to the extent that you did it to one of these brothers of Mine, even the least of them, you did it to Me.'*

Then He will also say to those on His left, 'Depart from Me, accursed ones, into the eternal fire which has been prepared for the devil and his angels; for I was hungry, and you gave Me nothing to eat; I was thirsty, and you gave Me nothing to drink; I was a stranger, and you did not invite Me in; naked, and you did not clothe Me; sick, and in prison, and you did not visit Me. Then they themselves also will answer, 'Lord, when did we see You hungry, or thirsty, or a stranger, or naked, or sick, or in prison, and did not take care of You?' Then He will answer them, 'Truly I say to you, to the extent that you did not do it to one of the least of these, you did not do it to Me.' These will go away into eternal punishment, but the righteous into eternal life.

Revelation 20:11-14, *Then I saw a great white throne and Him who sat upon it, from whose presence earth and heaven fled away, and no place was found for them. And I saw the dead, the great and the small, standing before the throne, and books were opened; and another book was opened, which is the book of life; and the dead were judged from the things which were written in the books, according to their deeds. And the sea gave up the dead which were in it, and death and Hades gave up the dead which were in them; and they were judged, every one of them according to their deeds. Then death and Hades were thrown into the lake of fire. This is the second death, the lake of fire.*

Some teach there are different judgements of which some have already been fulfilled, which may be true, but none of us know for certain how all of this is going to happen exactly since we are NOT the judge; Jesus is, thank God. However, to put the word 'final' or 'last' on anything intrinsic, dealing with the Kingdom of God means; 'there will be no more of that ever in His Kingdom.' Yet, we know that the Kingdom of God is an everlasting and eternal Kingdom and of His Government and peace there will be no end, so making judgements will not end. Some teach that this was the final judgement on the law and referred to the destruction of the temple in 70 A.D. and that could be also.

Jesus also taught His disciples that they would rule with Him, and He would entrust them with, and appoint unto them, a kingdom. Also, if we are kings and priests, then there will be righteous judgements being made throughout eternity. So, my point is, it is a myth to say there will be a 'final judgement' in the Kingdom since it is not in Scripture. How everything goes down in the future, and what we will be doing, along with the Godhead throughout eternity, is conjecture at best. I am just glad to be a son and part of the Father's Kingdom; and according to 1John 4:17-18, *By this, love is perfected with us, so that we may have confidence in the day of judgment*; (because as He is, so also are we in this world). *There is no fear in love; but perfect love casts out fear, because fear involves punishment, and the one who fears is not perfected in love.* I have no fear on judgement day, for I am as Jesus is on the Earth.

Myth #24
The age of accountability.

Many of us have heard about the age of accountability and how God gives grace to children who have not comprehended the gospel or have not yet learned to discern between good and evil. This idea comes from the Hebrew mindset that a child was not 'grown' or considered an adult until 12 years old, where they go through a ceremony which makes them 'sons of the law' and considered an adult. I personally am not against the idea, but what do you do with someone that suffers from mental problems and at the age of 40, still can't comprehend, or a deaf mute who cannot hear it or confess it; is there extended grace for them?

Many in the early church believed like Augustine at the council of Carthage in 418; "If a child was not baptized as an infant, they are suffering in hell with the damned' (but more mildly put). The Catholic church changed this in the middle ages to 'they were not thrown into hell but were in a place of limbo where God's presence was not'. Then, men like John Calvin from the post-reformation era was reported as supposedly saying that, 'hell is riddled with infants.' Which would not surprise me since he believed in limited atonement, and that only the elect was atoned for and not the whole World. So, if a child died as a baby, and they were not predestined as the elect, then they are being tormented in hell for eternity, which is repulsive to any sane person. The only Scripture that throws a monkey wrench in this idea of an age of accountability is found in 2 Chronicles 36:9, *Jehoiachin was eight years old when he became king, and he reigned three months and ten days in Jerusalem, and he did evil in the sight of the LORD.* So, here is an 8-year-old doing evil and God was displeased, so the question for us is, "How do we view God's mercy and justice in these situations?" Neither of these are easy questions and none of us are the judge or jury on these situations, nor do we have the definitive answer. We must leave that up to the character and mercy of Jesus, who the Father gave all judgement to, and trust His wisdom.

This has been a theological argument for a few thousand years and yet there is NO Scripture to define it; the truth is, we really do not know. Our job is to proclaim the 'Good News' so thru faith, people of all ages will trust, believe and have boldness with no fear on judgement day. I choose to believe that God in His infinite mercy and grace will decide those things correctly, and I do not believe that children are being tortured period. I am also just glad that none of us get to decide, because we would probably screw it up.

Myth #25
Three Kings came to Bethlehem and gave Him gifts at the manger.

The nativity scenes in front of many houses and churches around Christmas time normally depict Mary, Joseph, baby Jesus, shepherds, animals and three kings or wise men. Although these are not bad in themselves and are good reminders to everyone what Christmas is a celebration of, they are NOT Scripturally correct. First, they were not out in a stable or barn (we dealt with that in myth #22) and the King's or wise men or Magi, as some translations call them, did not show up until months later.

The story is found in Matt. 2:1-12, *Now after Jesus was born in Bethlehem of Judea in the days of Herod the king, magi from the east arrived in Jerusalem,* saying *"Where is He who has been born King of the Jews? For we saw His star in the east and have come to worship Him." When Herod the king heard this, he was troubled, and all Jerusalem with him. Gathering together all the chief priests and scribes of the people, he inquired of them where the Messiah was to be born. They said to him, "In Bethlehem of Judea; for this is what has been written by the prophet: 'AND YOU, BETHLEHEM, LAND OF JUDAH, ARE BY NO MEANS LEAST AMONG THE LEADERS OF JUDAH; FOR OUT OF YOU SHALL COME FORTH A RULER, WHO WILL*

SHEPHERD MY PEOPLE ISRAEL' Then Herod secretly called the magi and determined from them the exact time the star appeared. And he sent them to Bethlehem and said, "Go and search carefully for the Child; and when you have found Him, report to me, so that I too may come and worship Him." After hearing the king, they went their way; and the star, which they had seen in the east, went on before them until it came and stood over the place where the Child was. When they saw the star, they rejoiced exceedingly with great joy. After coming into the house, they saw the Child with Mary, His mother; and they fell to the ground and worshiped Him. Then, opening their treasures, they presented to Him gifts of gold, frankincense, and myrrh. And having been warned by God in a dream not to return to Herod, the magi left for their own country by another way.

    This tells us that they traveled far from the East and came to Herod to ask about the newborn King, probably assuming He was at the palace. Then, Herod has his philosophers look up in the scrolls where the messiah was to be born and it was Bethlehem, so they started out for Bethlehem, but then it says the star appeared and led them to the HOUSE not stable; where the child (not the baby) was; it never says they went to Bethlehem. Joseph and Mary lived in Nazareth and not Bethlehem, they only went to Bethlehem for the census. It would be perfectly logical that after Jesus was born, they went home to their house in Nazareth

This was at least in Jesus' first two years from birth, because Herod had all the male children two years old and under killed, and if Jesus would have been in Bethlehem, they might not have had enough time to flee to Egypt, but they would have enough time to flee from Nazareth, which was a ways from Jerusalem. The wise men brought the child Jesus three gifts which is where the idea of there being three of them comes from, even though some traditions teach it was as many as twelve. We really do not know from Scripture how many there were, even though according to some traditions and legend there were three and their names were Gaspar, Melchior and Balthazar, but that is conjecture at best.

The point of this myth, 'that there were three kings who came to a manger in Bethlehem' is NOT true. However, wise Kings today still come and bow before Him and give Him their gold; a type of their best which was associated with Kings and Lordship; Frankincense is a type of worship; for it was used as incense in worship. Myrrh is a type of our life, anointing, and death; for it was used in the anointing oil as well as to embalm a dead body. So just give Christ your life and your best today and watch what He will do with it.

Myth #26
There are streets of gold in Heaven.

Many of us have heard either from family, church, songs, or from tradition that Heaven has streets of gold. Now the only thing that we have that lets us know anything about Heaven is the Scriptures and they say NOTHING about golden streets. The Scriptures do talk about the 'New Jerusalem' in Revelation 21:21 and that the city has 'A Street' of gold, along with gates of pearls and many other precious jewels, but it says the city came down from Heaven OUT of God and not that it IS heaven. The context of Revelation 21:9, *Then one of the seven angels who had the seven bowls full of the seven last plagues came and spoke with me, saying, 'Come here, I will show you the bride, the wife of the lamb.'* 'The Lambs wife' is speaking about the bride, the 'Lambs wife' who is adorned in jewels and likened to a holy city as well as the Tabernacle of God that is now among men.

One of the descriptions of the new Jerusalem in the Old Testament is found in Isaiah 49:14-18 and it describes the city and the last verse says, *But Zion said, 'The Lord has forsaken me, And the Lord has forgotten me. Can a woman forget her nursing child and have no compassion on the son of her womb? Even these may forget, but I will not forget you. Behold, I have inscribed you on the palms of*

My hands; Your walls are continually before me. Your builders hurry; Your destroyers and devastators will depart from you. Lift up your eyes and look around; All of them gather together, they come to you. As I live, declares the Lord, You will surely put on all of them as jewels and bind them on as a bride.

Proverbs 31:10, *An excellent wife, who can find? For her worth is far above jewels.* Scriptures use the metaphor of jewels to describe the beloved in the Song of Songs as well as Proverbs. The book of Revelation is full of hyperbole, metaphor, and simile, because it is apocalyptic language that is rarely literal. Any time you interpret the word 'city' it is talking about people and not buildings or streets. If you take all of the people out of your city, it is no longer considered a city but a ghost town. Plus, Revelation 3:12 says that the overcomer will have a name written on their forehead, New Jerusalem; maybe this City is a people and not just a place.

Jesus told us that we are a city set on a hill, and Hebrews 12:22-23 says, *But you have come to Mount Zion and to the city of the living God, the heavenly Jerusalem, and to myriads of angels, the general assembly and church of the firstborn who are enrolled in heaven, and to God, the Judge of all, and to the spirits of the righteous* made perfect,

The New Jerusalem not only has 'A' street, but it is a transparent one that you can see through. It has foundations built on the apostles and the prophets, which sounds a whole lot more like the church than anything else. It is also 1,500 miles high and wide, which if you take that literally, it would stretch to the stratosphere, and is not impossible with God, but who knows what purpose that would have? So, however you interpret the book of Revelation, whether you believe it is literal or not, you still cannot find golden streets, but a golden street, which is the point of this myth.

Myth #27
'I' am the 'church', so I do not need to attend a corporate gathering.

I have heard this statement many times, especially over the last decade. I understand that people are tired of, finished with, and not interested in much of what has been considered 'church.' However, there is no 'I' in Church, and even though we individually are the Temple (naos; inner sanctuary) of the Holy Spirit, we are NOT individually 'the church'. The word translated church is the Greek word 'Ecclesia' which means 'called out one'S' (a congregation, an assembly) and in Acts 19 it was translated as the assembly of the Athenian government.

All through the Old Testament, this word in the Septuagint (Greek rendering of the whole Bible) was also consistent with the New Testament; meaning of a group of people called together for a purpose. It is never used to describe an individual, but a group of individuals who have gathered together to make decisions as well as worship in some form. In many of the cultures in the East, especially Hebrew culture, it was not considered a Synagogue until there were at least 10 men present. The word 'Synagogue' also started out meaning 'the congregation' or 'the people gathering' but by the time of Jesus it had become also 'the place' where the people would gather, and neither Jesus or Paul preached against that but instead frequented them often.

Now I want all of you to know that this myth is not about how you choose to gather or what you call it; whether it's in a large building, a house, a storefront, a coffee house, bowling alley, gym, restaurant, or a bar. The point is that we gather, and that gathering is the church and not just me and Jesus at my house with no one else. There is more to this meaning from a Kingdom government side, but my point to this myth is that no individual person is the church by themselves.

Myth #28
Everyone has always had a Bible to read and study.

What we call the 'Bible' was not compiled together as Old and New Testaments and canonized and recognized until sometime after 390 A.D. or so. There is a debate on some of this and some argue about which Bible, since the first ones included Apocryphal books which total 80 rather than 66 books. This includes the 1611 King James version. I was also taught that the 80 books were a Catholic thing and that it was changed during the reformation. I found this was not true and it actually was 80 books until the 1880's. Some of the reformers taught out of the 80 books (except Martin Luther who ripped James out, lol). My point in this myth is not to argue about translations or which one is right or wrong, or who authorized the canonization of the Scriptures, or who decided what was in and what was out. What I want all of us to understand, who live in the 21st century, is that from the times of Jesus up to nearly the 20th century, the literacy rate was on average 3-10 percent, and in a few areas as high as 25 percent. Most of the Bibles available were in Latin and very few could actually read it.

In the first few centuries, the apostles did not walk around with tablets and parchments. Much of what was learned by the people was given orally and by memory. We who live now have Bibles in many translations on our book shelves or in our phones, and yet for the major part of church history this was not available to the regular Joe on the street. Only a few educated or wealthy people had copies. In most communities, the Bible they heard from was locked up in the local Parrish and read at mass. Until the reformation and the Wittenburg press, it was not in the language of the people

When we argue today about the Bible, it is because of the plethora of information we now have and yet for most of church history, believers had to rely on whatever they were taught and the indwelling Holy Spirit to help them know what was right. We are blessed to live today and have the Scriptures available to us, but I also wonder how much simpler it was in the early church to simply love as He loved in community, teach the forgiveness of sins, pray for each other, and heal the sick without all the arguing of doctrine.

Myth #29
The Holy Spirit came from Heaven on the day of Pentecost.

I have heard this said my whole life growing up in the Pentecostal church, but it does not say this in the passage that is quoted, Acts 2:1-4, *When the day of Pentecost had come, they were all together in one place. And suddenly there came from heaven a noise like a violent rushing wind, and it filled the whole house where they were sitting. And there appeared to them tongues as of fire distributing themselves, and they rested on each one of them. And they were all filled with the Holy Spirit and began to speak with other tongues, as the Spirit was giving them utterance.*

It does say that a 'sound' (a report, noise, a blast) came from Heaven as 'simile' (a figure of speech describing something using like or as) a rushing mighty wind (breath, wind, or breeze) similar to Adam who walked with God in the cool (wind, breeze) of the day. One translation says, 'a bearing forceful puff'. The 'sound' filled the room and tongues AS of fire sat on them and they were filled (fulfilled, completed, accomplished, supplied, maximum and full extent) and began to speak in tongues (languages) as the Spirit gave utterance.

In John 20:22, Jesus breathed on His disciples after His Resurrection when He walked into a closed room and said, *Receive the Holy Spirit.* This gives an inference in the Greek language as 'receive NOW the Holy Spirit'. Jesus breathed the Holy Spirit into them before He ascended and then to fulfill Scriptures and the feast of Pentecost, He released a breath (a blast, or word from Heaven) just like the Godhead did in Genesis chapter one in creating this World; and it 'the breath' or 'word' caused a release and maximum filling of the Spirit 'out of them' then 'clothed' or 'came UPON them' and ignited a new creation.

Jesus said in John 7:37-38 *Now on the last day, the great day of the feast, Jesus stood and cried out, saying, 'If anyone is thirsty, let him come to Me and drink. He who believes in Me, as the Scripture said, from his innermost being will flow rivers of living water'.* When Jesus breathed on them He was now glorified. Peter in Acts 2:17 goes on to quote Joel 2 but not exactly, for Joel 2:28 *says, It will come about after this that I will pour out My Spirit on all mankind; And your sons and daughters will prophesy, Your old men will dream dreams, Your young men will see visions.*

Yet, Peter says in Acts 2:17, *And it shall be in the last days, God says, That I will pour fourth of my Spirit on all mankind, and your sons and your daughters shall prophesy, and your young men shall see visions, and your old men will dream dreams.* NKJV and the NASB says, 'pour forth OF my Spirit.' In other words, it is not God just pouring out His Spirit from Heaven but pouring forth 'and out' of His Spirit, that was already in them, because Jesus had poured and breathed His Spirit into them already.

Luke 24:49, *And behold, I am sending forth the promise of My Father upon you; but you are to stay in the city until you are clothed with power from on high.* Jesus said 'that which was coming' was a clothing of power from Heaven and not the Holy Spirit. Acts 1:8 says, *but you will receive power when the Holy Spirit has come upon* (throughout, having charge of, all around you). So, it is a work of the Holy Spirit. My point in this myth is, it is coming from inside of you and not the sky, as a believer. So, am I nitpicking? Perhaps, lol, but I have watched way too many people go to altars looking for something to drop on them from the sky and leave disappointed, and disillusioned, which has caused them to throw away and reject an amazing gift that God wants to have flow out of them. By not understanding that God was doing it from the inside and pouring out OF His Spirit. Ephesians 3:20, *Now to Him who is able to do far more abundantly beyond all that we ask or think, according to the power* (dunamis) *that works with 'IN' us.* Not what is going to drop down from Heaven. *We have been* (past tense) *blessed with every spiritual blessing in the Heavenly Christ.* according to Ephesians 1:3. Some translations say in heavenly 'places' but it is written in 'italics' which means it has been added into the Scripture by the translators. I want to encourage all of you to be clothed with power and yield to the Holy Spirit, who is already in you, and by faith, let Him fill and complete you from the inside out, and be clothed with Jesus as Paul said in Romans 13.

Myth #30
The disciples were in the upper room on the day of Pentecost.

    I grew up singing a song called, "O Lord, send the power just now" It started with "They were in an upper chamber, they were all in one accord, when the Holy Ghost descended as was promised by the Lord." I have been to churches who named themselves 'Upper Room Ministries' based on the idea that the 120 were in an upper chamber of a house when the Holy Spirit manifested. This comes from Acts 1:13, *When they had entered the city, they went up to the upper room where they were staying; that is, Peter and John and James and Andrew, Philip and Thomas, Bartholomew and Matthew, James the son of Alphaeus, and Simon the Zealot, and Judas the son of James.*

    This shows the disciples along with Mary and Jesus' brothers along with a few other women went to an upper room where the disciples were staying (notice not everyone, just the disciples stayed there) to pray. However, in Acts 2:1-2, *When the day of Pentecost had come, they were all together in one place and suddenly there came from heaven a noise like a violent rushing wind, and it filled the whole house where they were sitting.* It says they were in one accord and in 'one place' and the sound filled the house (abode- or any building or structure is the way that word was used then, which could be an actual house or a larger building).

The 120 would have been hard pressed to find an upper chamber of a home to all fit in at that time in Jerusalem, but Luke who is the author of Acts tells us in Luke 24:52-53, *And they, after worshiping Him, returned to Jerusalem with great joy, and were continually in the temple praising God.* So, they were already making it a daily thing to go to the temple and worship, and it was full of porches and large rooms around the courts. The disciples, as Jews, would have been at that time of morning at the temple presenting themselves at the feast of 'Shavuot' as Deut. 16:16 instructs, *Three times a year, all your males shall appear before the LORD your God, in the place which he chooses: at the Feast of Unleavened Bread, and at the Feast of Weeks, and at the Feast of Booths. They shall not appear before the LORD empty-handed.*

They gathered together to pray and worship when the Holy Spirit manifested out of them with a new language (glossolalia). It says that Jews from many different countries and dialects heard them magnifying God in their own language, and thought they were drunk. This could not have been at a house in an upper room because no one would have heard except a few neighbors. However, in the temple courts, where thousands were coming to worship at one of the high holy days, that would have caused quite a stir which would cause the people to ask, "What does this mean?" Peter then stood up to bring explanation to a multitude of people of which at least three- thousand were present, because at least three-thousand were added to the church that day, not including women and children. There is no way that three-thousand people would have fit in the narrow streets of Jerusalem outside of a house.

The temple also had large pools for immersion which Peter also said, *Repent and be baptized* (immersed) in Acts 2:38, and God said in Malachi 3:1, That He would come suddenly to His temple, *Behold, I am going to send My messenger, and he will clear the way before Me. And the Lord, whom you seek, will suddenly come to His temple; and the messenger of the covenant, in whom you delight, behold, He is coming, says the LORD of hosts.* Which makes sense that 'The new temple' (the church) would be in the old temple, and that would be a beautiful picture of that verse.

My point is, the disciples were sleeping and staying in the upper room, but that is NOT where Acts 2:1-2 took place, but instead was in the temple courts because the day of Pentecost had now FULLY come.

Myth #31
There is a mansion in Heaven just for you after you die.

I like to refer to much of what we have been taught as 'song book theology' since many of our beliefs have come more from songs we sang then actual right interpretation of Scripture. I grew up singing 'Mansion over the Hilltop' which is not bad in itself, but any example we have of anyone being caught up into Heaven, in Scripture, there were no buildings except the temple or God's house. Whether it was Isaiah, Ezekiel, Daniel, Paul or John the Revelator, everyone saw, 'a building, people, angels, elders, animals and beasts' as well as John seeing a city, which is people and not buildings, because without people it is not a city but a ghost town. We get this idea from ONE verse which you normally can-NOT make a doctrine out of one verse, but must have agreement with at least 2 or 3. John 14:2, *In my Father's house are many 'mansions* (KJV) 'dwelling places' in the NASB and in most other translations, which is a better translation from the Greek language.

What I want to point out is, it is in the Father's house not ours, and Jesus was using the Jewish imagery of a Father's house which was where the extended family lived, for they would add rooms as the family grew through birth and marriage. This is also a picture of Him preparing us as His house for Him, this is not about US getting a big house if we are good kids, or if we suffer down here. Know you not, know you not, that you are the temple of the Holy Spirit? We are the rooms and dwelling places that He is building for Him. Psalm 46:4, *There is a river whose streams make glad the city of God, the Holy dwelling places of the Most High.* We are those dwelling places.

Paul tells us in Ephesians 2:21-22, *in whom the whole building, being fitted together, is growing into a holy temple in the Lord, in whom you also are being built together into a dwelling of God in the Spirit.* 1 Peter 2:5, *You also, as living stones are being built up as a spiritual house for a holy priesthood, to offer up spiritual sacrifices acceptable to God through Jesus Christ.* There are many examples that show that this is NOT just for us but for Him. Plus, once Heaven is manifested fully on Earth, then you will not need a house there but here; this infers according to 2 Corinthians 5 of how our old bodies are a tent that we will put off and put on new dwelling and clothes that are being prepared for us.

Our glorified bodies could also be a meaning to this, according to some scholars, and when all of this takes place; which there has been much discussion about through the years. However, my point in this myth is for us to not look for a pie in the sky kind of theology but realize that Heavenly

Father has a lot of room in His house and family and He is preparing us for Himself and not something just for me.

Myth #32
Jesus and the apostles 'publicly' taught that we must be born again.

When I was growing up in church and I would meet people from other denominations and churches, we did not ask each other if we were Christians, we would ask, "Are you a 'born again' Christian?" This of course comes from John 3:1-8 or so, *Now there was a man of the Pharisees, named Nicodemus, a ruler of the Jews; this man came to Jesus by night and said to Him, 'Rabbi, we know that You have come from God as a teacher; for no one can do these signs that You do unless God is with him.' Jesus answered and said to him, 'Truly, truly, I say to you, unless one is born again he cannot see the kingdom of God.' Nicodemus said to Him, 'How can a man be born when he is old? He cannot enter a second time into his mother's womb and be born, can he?' Jesus answered, 'Truly, truly, I say to you, unless one is born of water and Spirit he cannot enter into the kingdom of God. That which is born of flesh is flesh, and that which is born of the Spirit is Spirit. Do not be amazed that I said to you, 'You must be born again.' The wind blows where it wishes, and you hear the sound of it, but do not know where it comes from and where it is going; so is everyone who is born of the Spirit.'*

Here Jesus is having a late-night discussion with a Pharisee who is asking Him how He teaches, knows what He knows, and manifests the signs that He does. Jesus responds, "Unless you are born again you cannot see the Kingdom of God." Now many translations say, 'born again' which is not necessarily bad, but the original Greek along with most literal translations say, 'born from above.' This gives a different connotation. 'Born from above' gives the source of the regeneration where 'born again' does not really reflect the source.

A new destiny needs a new origin which is the Kingdom of God, which is what Jesus came preaching. He told Pilate, 'My Kingdom is not from (of) here, or its source is not Earthly but Heavenly.' I remember my spiritual mother in the faith, Dr. Fuschia Pickett, saying in the early 90's, "Why is it that one of our cardinal doctrines in the protestant church is 'being born again' when Jesus NEVER publicly preached it? Jesus had spoken it to one man late at night and only John recorded it; maybe he was the only one that heard it because he was always laying on Jesus' chest and he got woke up. It was only recorded once." It certainly got me thinking; she never said it shouldn't be taught either. The only other time it is used is in a different Greek phrase in 1 Peter 1:22-23, *Since you have in obedience to the truth purified your souls for a sincere love of the brethren, fervently love one another from the heart, for you have been born again not of a seed which is perishable but imperishable, that is, through the living and enduring word of God.* It was over 20 years ago that this thought had challenged me; since doctrines are predominantly built on at least two or three 'witness' not on just one verse. Also, the apostles never went around proclaiming, 'you must be born again' but they instead preached, *Peter said to them, 'Repent and each of you be baptized in the name of Jesus Christ for the forgiveness of your sins; and you will receive the gift of the Holy Spirit'* Acts 2:38. When you check church history, the term 'born again' became prominent after the reformation and this was mainly in the protestant evangelical world, to distinguish between those who received Christ by faith compared to those who were baptized as infants.

Now is it a big deal to tell someone to be born again? No, but it is more than saying a prayer which the apostles never taught; and it was about a new life, new King, new government, and something you would be willing to give your life for. Jesus was also talking to a Pharisee and a Jew who had been taught that being the natural seed of Abraham meant that you were in the Kingdom by natural birth and bloodline. Jesus then is telling Nicodemus to do what He does, he had to come out of religion and be born from above, and that his natural birth and lineage meant nothing because we all need Jesus, who came from Heaven and not Earth.

In saying all of this, my point to this myth is, there is nothing wrong with the phrase, but don't teach it like it is THE thing that Jesus and the apostles taught because it wasn't. The church fathers never taught it for nearly 1,500 years; if it had been translated differently we would probably not be having this conversation, lol.

Myth #33
The animals that went in to Noah's ark were 2 of every kind, both male and female.

Many of us were taught this correctly in Sunday school, but I bet if you were to ask most church attenders if the above statement were true, they would say yes. Now the animals were taken in by twos and pairs, but that was only the unclean animals. God instructed Noah that the clean animals were to be taken by seven, in pairs. This is found in Genesis 7:1-5, *Then the LORD said to Noah, 'Enter the ark, you and all your household, for you alone have seen to be righteous before Me in this time. You shall take with you of every clean animal by sevens, male and female, to keep offspring alive on the face of all the earth. For after seven more days, I will send rain on the earth forty days and forty nights; and I will blot out from the face of the land every living thing that I have made.' Noah did according to all that the Lord had commanded him.* This is found in every translation of the Scriptures. God distinguishes between the clean and unclean, as well as the birds of the air, and then gives the instructions of how and what to do.

The flood story is full of wonderful hyperbole and metaphor of Christ's redemptive work for us, and down through history the flood story has been a topic of much debate. Some teach that it was literal, and some teach it was myth or a story conveying a truth, I have studied both sides and both make valid points. The ark has never been found, so the debate will probably rage on which is why I choose to focus on the rainbow and the covenant that God would not destroy the Earth again. Also, the ark landed on a Mount called Ararat which means 'the reversing of a curse' This is the good news in the story, as it was a prefiguring of what our savior would do in the future.

Myth #34
'The Lord's Prayer' is how the Lord prayed.

The Lord's prayer, as it has been called, is found in Matthew 6:9-1, *Pray, then, in this way: Our Father who is in heaven, hallowed be Your name. Your kingdom come, Your will be done, on earth as it is in heaven; Give us this day our daily bread. And forgive us our debts, as we also have forgiven our debtors. And do not lead us into temptation but deliver us from evil. For Yours is the kingdom and the power and the glory forever. Amen.* It is also in many of our Bibles (stated in captions above this teaching of Jesus to His disciples about prayer).

The disciples asked Jesus to teach them how to pray the way John taught his disciples how to pray. Jesus then gives THEM this outline called, for some reason, 'the Lord's prayer' when it should probably be called 'the disciples prayer.' This was not a prayer that Jesus would pray to the Father because Jesus had no trespasses to be forgiven for, and He was the daily bread in flesh as well as THE will of the Father.

We are told in 2 Corinthians 5:21, *He made Him who knew no sin to be sin on our behalf, so that we might become the righteousness of God in Him*, as well as Hebrews 4:15, *For we do not have a high priest who cannot sympathize with our weaknesses, but One who has been tempted in all things as we are, yet without sin.* The real 'Lord's prayer' is found in John 17:1-5, *Jesus spoke these things; and lifting up His eyes to heaven, He said, 'Father, the hour has come; glorify Your Son, that the Son may glorify You, even as You gave Him authority over all flesh, that to all whom You have given Him, He may give eternal life. This is eternal life, that they may know You, the only true God, and Jesus Christ whom You have sent. I glorified You on the earth, having accomplished the work which You have given Me to do. Now, Father, glorify Me together with Yourself, with the glory which I had with You before the world was.* He is praying to the Father for His disciples as well as for all of us who would believe their message about Him.

Now is there anything necessarily wrong with calling it the Lord's prayer? No, because He taught it as a prayer, but this myth is about whether it is how He prayed, which it was not about how He prayed, but how the disciples should pray. This is also a template and not THE way to pray but simply a good outline on how to get started, so please just pray, lol.

Myth #35
Adam and Eve were tempted to eat an apple in the Garden of Eden.

Eve eating an apple has been the picture that many of us have seen through the years when shown a picture of the fall of man in the garden. Now Adam and Eve probably had eaten an apple at one time or another, since God gave them every other tree in the garden to eat. However, the fruit of the tree of the knowledge of good and evil was probably not an apple, since a tree can only bear fruit after its own kind. This comes from Genesis 3:5-7, *For God knows that in the day you eat from it your eyes will be opened, and you will be like God, knowing good and evil. When the woman saw that the tree was good for food, and that it was a delight to the eyes, and that the tree was desirable to make one wise, she took from its fruit and ate; and she gave also to her husband with her and he ate.* (which describes the exchange between the serpent and eve and that she desired the fruit of that tree, then ate and gave it to her husband, Adam, who was with her.)

There are different theories of what the fruit was, some believe it was figs because it says they used fig leaves to cover themselves, once they realized they were naked, and figs were a long-standing symbol of female sexuality dealing with the fruit of the womb. Jesus also cursed the fig tree that was not bearing fruit which has a lot of symbolism in its meaning. Some teach it was pomegranates, while others teach it was grapes.

The truth is, we do NOT really know, which the point of this myth is, but most Bible scholars do not believe it was an apple. The truth is that the tree and its fruit caused them to know good and evil or sin and that produced the mess that this World is in. I do not believe that the fruit is something that is a natural thing (that is here today) to physically be able to eat; it is either a metaphor for something else or it is a fruit still in the garden that is hidden, but who really knows. So, remember, an apple a day keeps the doctor away, lol.

Myth #36
Females are not allowed to speak, teach or minister in a church gathering.

This subject has been a debate in the church for generations because of a few verses that the apostle Paul shared in two of his epistles. There are whole books written on just this subject, so I will not be able to give an exhaustive study, but I believe it is very simple, because of a few words that should have been translated differently. The first one is found in 1 Timothy 2:12-13, *But I do not allow a woman to teach or exercise authority over a man, but to remain quiet. For it was Adam who was first created, and then Eve.* As well as 1 Corinthians 14:34-35, *The women are to keep silent in the churches; for they are not permitted to speak, but are to subject themselves, just as the Law also says. If they desire to learn anything, let them ask their own husbands at home; for it is improper for a woman to speak in church.* 1 Timothy 2:12-13 in the Youngs literal translation says this, *A woman, I do not suffer to teach, nor to rule a husband, but to be in quietness.*

Let me start by saying that I believe the context of these are dealing with husbands and wives and not males and females. The word for man is also translated husband and the word for woman is also translated wife, and in both of these instances, the marriage relationship is brought up;

and in Timothy he talks about the relationship of Adam and Eve and then talks about child-bearing which would not be spoken to just a female, but married ones, since this is plural in the Greek. Paul also tells us in Galatians 3:28, *There is neither Jew nor Greek, there is neither slave nor free man, there is neither male nor female; for you are all one in Christ Jesus.* We are also told in Acts 2:17 that God would pour out His Spirit on all flesh and your daughters would prophesy; *And it shall be in the last days, God says, 'That I will pour forth of My Spirit on all mankind; and your sons and your daughters shall prophesy, and your young men shall see visions, and your old men shall dream dreams.*

In Acts 21:9 it tells us of Phillips daughters who prophesied... *Now this man had four virgin daughters who were prophetesses.* (Which is a word that means 'to proclaim' as well as 'to teach' while inspired) plus, in 1 Corinthians 11:4-5, women are told to cover their heads, while praying and prophesying, and it is in the context of their church gatherings. *Every man who has something on his head while praying or prophesying disgraces his head. But every woman who has her head uncovered while praying or prophesying disgraces her head, for she is one and the same as the woman whose head is shaved.*

In Romans 16:1 Paul honors Phoebe, a deaconess, *I commend to you our sister Phoebe, a deaconess of the church which is at Cenchrea*, and then also honors Priscilla and Aquila in Vs. 3-4, *Greet Priscilla and Aquila, my fellow workers in Christ Jesus, who for my life risked their own necks, to whom not only do I give thanks, but also all the churches of Gentiles*, and John writes a whole epistle to the elect lady in 2 John, *The elder to the elect lady and her children, whom I love in the truth, and not only I but also all who know the truth for the sake of the truth which abides in us and will be with us forever. Grace, Mercy and peace will be with us, from God the Father and from Jesus Christ the Son of the Father, in truth and love. I was very glad to find some of your children walking in truth, just as we have received commandment to do from the Father.*

So obviously, Paul was not being literal as in 'females' cannot let out a peep in church, but instead he is dealing with wives who were not submitted to their husbands or were usurping authority and being controlling and disruptive (also study the culture of the Corinthians who worshiped a female deity, it will help).

The Christian faith, and especially Jesus, was very pro females; as a matter of fact, the first apostle 'sent one' of the Resurrection, was a woman, Mary. For years, I have had men say to me that women should not lead or be given any authority, and my response is that the only gender that God gave authority in the earth realm is a female, which is why the church is called His bride and wife and not His husband.

Any time we are still promoting the men's club, when it comes to church leadership, it is a good sign that we are still under the law, for it was under Aaron that it was fathers to sons. Paul flips the switch when He exhorts Timothy's mother and grandmother as his influences which had never been done in Scripture until then, because the priesthood has now changed; for we are now in a New Covenant with a new priesthood that see's all 'as one' in Christ. So, gentlemen, please stop being intimidated by the ladies and release them into their purpose and callings and watch the church flourish.

Myth #37
The Bible was authored and written by God alone.

I thank God I live in a day where the Scriptures are readily available. During the first 1,600 years or so of the church this was not a reality. Most people were illiterate and along with Scripture being mainly in Latin, this made it so very few could read them; along with the fact there were also very few copies available.

So, first and most important, I want everyone to know that I LOVE THE SCRIPTURES; I teach them, read them, live by them, study them on a regular basis, and I believe God inspired them. Now having said that, I have also heard many people say that God is the author and He wrote the Bible. The Scriptures never claim this; neither did the church fathers or Jewish Rabbis, who would argue for years with Scribes and other sects over the meaning of the Torah and how to interpret it.

We know that the Bible was co-authored; it was MEN who wrote as they were inspired by God and as He breathed upon it and them, 2 Timothy 3:16, *All Scripture is inspired by God and profitable for teaching, for reproof, for correction, for training in righteousness.* And 2 Peter 1:21, *For no prophecy was ever made by an act of human will, but men moved by the Holy Spirit spoke from God.* This does not make it any less powerful or less important, but it does help us understand how some of the things written was man putting their culture and opinion in at times.

There are more than 40 different authors who wrote and some of them added their own thoughts; like Paul saying I am writing this by permission or he is sharing his opinion in 1 Corinthians 7:25-40 or so, *Now concerning virgins I have no command of the Lord, but I give an opinion as one who by the mercy of the Lord is trustworthy. I think then that this is good in view of the present distress, that it is good for a man to remain as he is. Are you bound to a wife? Do not seek to be released. Are you released from a wife? Do not seek a wife. But if you marry, you have not sinned; and if a virgin marries, she has not sinned. Yet such will have trouble in this life, and I am trying to spare you. But this I say, brethren, the tie has been shortened, so that from now on those who have wives should be as though they had none; and those who weep, as though they did not weep; and those who rejoice, as though they did not rejoice; and those who buy, as though they did not possess; and those who use the world as though they did not make full use of it; for the form of this world is passing away. But I want you to be free from concern. One who is unmarried is concerned about the things of the Lord, how he may please the Lord; but one who is married is concerned about the things of the world, how he may please his wife, and his interests are divided. The woman who is unmarried, and the virgin, is concerned about the things of the Lord, that she may be holy both in body and spirit; but one who is married is concerned about the things of the world, how she may please her husband. This I say for your own benefit; not to put a restraint upon you but to promote what is appropriate and to secure undistracted devotion to the Lord. But if any man thinks that he is acting unbecomingly toward his virgin daughter, if she is past her youth, and if it must be so, let him do what he wishes, he does not sin; let her marry. But he who stands firm in his heart, being under no constraint, but has authority over his own will, and has decided this in his own heart, to keep his own virgin daughter, he will do well. So then both he who gives his own virgin daughter in marriage does well, and he who does not give her in marriage will do better. A wife is bound as long as her husband lives; but if her husband is dead, she is free to be married to whom she wishes, only in the Lord. But in my opinion, she is happier if she remains as she is; and I think that I also have the Spirit of God.*

    This did not mean what He said was wrong, or less important, or that it disagreed with God, but just that it was his opinion and God had no problem with him writing it down. Some of them also wrote their own perceptions, even though Jesus would reinterpret them and even prove some of them wrong. Such as 'The Sermon on the Mount' saying, "You have heard said (or Moses said), but I say" and then gives the polar opposite view. In other words, 'Abba and I never said that, even though God had no problem with Moses writing it down.'

The Bible is also not 'A' book but 'a library' of 66 books or 80, if you embrace the Apocrypha; which recorded prophesies, history, stories, songs, poetry, facts, biographies, and even personal greetings. We are told by Paul in Romans 15:4, *For whatever was written in earlier times was written for our instruction, so that through perseverance and the encouragement of the Scriptures we might have hope."* Paul said that we are co-laborers with Christ, and Jesus described the Holy Spirit as our comforter (paraclete or helper).

I want you to notice the Holy Spirit is not the 'doer' but the 'helper' so God has always chosen to partner with man on the Earth, and He did the same with the recording of the Scriptures as well as the canonizing of them. This myth is not about how all that came together or what translation is correct but was to simply debunk the idea that it was God alone, since He did not actually write it but did inspire, breath on, and co-author it, with man's help.

Myth #38
There is 'A' World leader who is called "The anti-Christ" in the Bible.

Many of us have either heard this in church, a sci-fi movie, a horror flick, or a book that we read. THE anti-Christ is coming, or like many of us have been told, he has been alive for the last 60 years at least, and any minute is about to jump on the scene. End-time teachers have called everyone from Hitler, to Mussolini, to Saddam Hussein, to Presidents Reagan, Clinton, Bush, and Obama, as well as some Spanish prince in Europe, the 'anti-Christ'. And now all the craze is that it is Islam and some leader who will arise from that religion. Many teachers have taken Scriptures from Daniel, Isaiah, Zechariah, and 2 Thessalonians to prove the coming of an anti-Christ person, and yet not one of those Scriptures say anti-Christ and it isn't even found at all in the book of Revelation.

The only time the phrase 'anti-Christ' is found in Scripture is in John's epistles. 1 John 2:18-22, *Children, it is the last hour; and just as you heard that antichrist is coming, even now many antichrists have appeared; from this we know that it is the last hour. They went out from us, but they were not really of us; for if they had been of us, the would have remained with us; but they went out, so that it would be shown that they all are not of us. But you have an anointing from the Holy One, and you all know. I have not written to you because you do not know the truth, but because you do know it and because no lie is of the truth. Who is the liar but the one who denies that Jesus is the Christ? This is the antichrist, the one who denies the Father and the Son.*

    The definite article in the Greek language for 'THE' is not found in the original text and many newer translations, like the NASB, just say anti-Christ is coming and they leave out 'the'. John, in the context of his 2 Epistle that mentions anti-Christ was refuting the Gnostic's, who were a group of people that did not believe in the incarnation or that Jesus actually came in the flesh as God. This is why it says in 2 John 7, *For MANY deceivers, have gone out into the world, those who do not acknowledge Jesus Christ as coming in the flesh. This is the deceiver and the anti-Christ.*

    The word anti-Christ in the Greek is 'antikhristos' (against Christ or the opposite of Christ) or to take the place of, and it nearly always referred to a system, group, spirit, or attitude, and not just a single individual. John also says, *He is anti-Christ that denies the Father and the Son,* as well as, *every spirit that does not confess Jesus is from God, this is the spirit of anti-Christ which you heard was coming and is NOW in the World already.* John was showing how to discern between false and true teachers and was making it very clear that this was historically happening in their lifetime.

This myth is not about trying to prove a certain eschatological view, but to simply show that from the Scriptures, it does NOT say anything about a 'single World leader' called THE 'anti-Christ' who is going to rule the Earth one day. Now there are Scriptures that people believe are talking about this or refers to it, but to prove it, you have to engage in exegetical gymnastics, conjecture, and eisegesis, especially since John said this spirit was already there in his day and that they were in the 'FINAL HOUR' and not just the last day.

So, whatever you choose to believe about this is not going to affect your salvation or your relationship with Jesus, but to definitively teach that anti-Christ is A person is theory at best. So, my friends, let's focus on 'THE CHRIST' and how 'He' is Lord and proclaim Him, rather than fret and worry about an individual who is the devils Damien seed, lol, who is going to come and try to rule someday.

Myth #39
Adam gave the dominion of the Earth to the devil when he sinned.

I've heard this taught for many years and I understand where many could get it, after all the devil took Jesus up on a mountain and showed Him all the Kingdoms of the World (not the Earth) that he said were his (he is of course the father of lies, lol). In the garden, God gave delegated authority to Adam (mankind) to rule the Earth realm of God's Kingdom through a grace and dominion mandate in Genesis 1:28, God *blessed them and God said to them, 'Be fruitful, and multiply and fill the Earth and subdue it; and rule over the fish of the sea and the birds of the sky and over every living thing that moves on the earth.'* Adam then rebelled and ate the forbidden fruit and brought sin, death, and chaos into the World and its system, but that did not change man's dominion of the Earth. God then warns of a flood that would be destructive on the Earth and only Noah and his family survive. They then get off the ark with the animals they were given dominion over; they worship, and God gives them the same mandate He gave Adam. In Genesis 9:7-20, Vs.7 *As for you, be fruitful and multiply; Populate the earth abundantly and multiply in it*; along with a covenant to never do it again

It is easy to assume that the devil took or was given that authority by mankind, which does not really make sense, because it was delegated authority from God, so the devil had no right or access to it without God giving it because this is still our Father's World. Psalm 115:16, *The heavens are the heavens of the Lord, but the Earth He has given to the sons of men.* The World and the Earth are not the same thing, we are told that the devil is the prince of the power of the air, but He is not the sovereign of the Earth. There are NO Scriptures that say the devil has the authority on the Earth, especially *when the Earth is the Lords and all it contains, the world, and those who dwell in it,* Psalm 24:1. Plus, Jesus defeated and destroyed the works of the devil at the cross and then said to His disciples in Matthew 28:18, *All authority has been given to Me in heaven and on the earth Heaven and Earth (because He had become a man, the last Adam).*

    The devil works on the Earth thru men for they are the ones that have been given the dominion, and it is the disease of sin, death, and fear as well as deception that gives him access to this World. In the same way, God works thru men to expand His family and His Kingdom on the Earth for we are co-laborers with Christ and the Holy Spirit is not the doer, but our helper. So just know that there has never been a time that the devil has ruled the Earth. That privilege was given to man by God, and it is man that screwed it up and it will take men empowered by God to help fix it.

Myth #40
God will tell some Christians someday, "Depart from me, you workers of iniquity, I never knew you." (Matthew 7:23)

This verse above almost all others got me saved at least 50 times when I was younger. When the Evangelist would get near the end of his message and say, "You can even preach, prophesy, cast out demons, and do miracles, but if you don't live and behave right, at the end of your life you won't make it in those pearly gates, for the Lord will say depart from me I never knew you." Thank God, in my 20's I learned how to properly interpret Scripture, and this was one of the first ones I studied because of how much condemnation it had put me under. First of all, Jesus, in this context, is talking about false prophets and their fruit (v15). He is not talking to Christians because there weren't any yet, because He had not died and inaugurated the new covenant.

His audience was made up of Jews who were under the Old Covenant, and He is dealing with them about the works they think will get them into the Kingdom. We see a picture of this in Acts 19:13-15 when a Jewish priest with His 7 sons were trying to cast out demons in the name of Jesus that Paul preaches; the demons speak and say, "Jesus we know and Paul we know, but who are you?" and then beat them good. They were not Christians, but Jews were trying to use His name who had no relationship with Him and were saying, "Lord, Lord" and trying to cast out demons in His name.

We know on this side of the cross that it is THE finished Work of Jesus that gets us in the Kingdom, and we access it by grace through faith and not thru works, (Eph. 2:8-*9) For by grace you have been saved through faith; and that not of yourselves, it is the gift of God; not as a result of works, so that no one may boast.* It does not mean that works are not good for we are not saved BY works, but we are saved FOR good works, but they flow out of our new nature and relationship with Jesus. This context starts in Matthew 7:10-27 and ends with the collapse of the house of those building on the sand rather than the rock; referring to THAT DAY which was in 70 A.D. when their temple (house) collapsed and their city which was not built on a revelation of Jesus, but the law, came tumbling down and GREAT was the fall of that house. Jesus is saying to them that if they do not hear and receive HIS words and obey the will of the Father which was to believe on Him, then their house will be swept away by a massive storm.

The Roman army led by Prince Titus nearly 40 years later, was that storm who leveled the house and the city to its foundations and Zion became a plowed field just like Micah prophesied. Jesus says, "Away from me you who practice lawlessness." in some of the other translations of this verse. This alone should cause those of us who live on this side of the cross, who were never given the law in the first place (especially as Gentiles) to question this being not written to us but for us. Plus, Jesus is not going to ever tell one of His sons or daughters, "I NEVER knew you." once you believe according to 1 John 4, You are as Jesus is on the Earth and you are in union with Him so, how could He ever tell you I NEVER knew you. It would be different if it would have said, "You never knew me." but it doesn't, for He will NEVER leave us or forsake us period.

    This myth is about whether that verse applies to Christians and it does not because Jesus will NEVER say to one of His, "Depart from me, I NEVER knew you.

Myth #41
Money is the root of all evil.

Most of us have heard this statement misquoted at one time or another and many believe it without really studying for themselves what it really says and means. The verse is found in 1 Timothy 6:10, *For the LOVE of money is 'A' root of all sorts of evil, and some by longing for it have wandered away from the faith and have pierced themselves with many griefs* (NASB). The verse actually says that it is the LOVE of money that leads to all kinds of griefs, evils, and destruction's (according to some other translations). So money, in itself, is not good or evil it is neutral, but our 'ATTITUDE' towards it is what causes problems.

It is when we long for wealth and money more than for Christ and the advancement of His Kingdom on the Earth, and when money becomes the goal rather than the Kingdom. God has no problem with us having money, but when money has us, it becomes an idol that will corrupt us. Money does not change anyone, but instead it is a magnifier of who one really is. If you were a jerk before you got money, you will probably now be a bigger jerk. If you were stingy before, you will probably be stingier after, and if you were generous before, you will be more generous after. This is why when someone wins the lottery, five years later many of them go broke because they weren't any good with money before they had it and so they were worse when they had a lot.

We are told in Ecclesiastes 10:19, *Money answers all things,* or in other words money talks, and what we spend our money on and what we seek speaks volumes of what is in our hearts. Jesus explains how where our heart is our treasure is also, so seek THE treasure which is Him and all the other will follow. I have heard said, "The greatest things in life are attracted and not pursued" so when we are simply loving Him rather than stuff, then the things we need will run us down. Otherwise we will see grief and sorrow and never be satisfied with money, so money is NOT evil, but how people use it can be.

Myth #42
Communion or the Lord's supper has always been a sacrament.

    The taking of or celebrating the Lords supper means different things to many, depending on how they were raised. For those raised in Catholicism or Orthodoxy, the entire service mainly revolves around the Supper (Eucharist) and is a Sacrament and very sacred. In Protestant and non-denominational churches, it is still a Sacrament but relegated to a back room or once a month, if that, even though some celebrate it differently. When I was growing up, it was something I was a little scared of because the focus was on examining yourself for sin (which I constantly found, lol) and if you don't you will die young. You don't dare take it if you are angry with someone, especially in the building, so you better make it right immediately or something horrible will happen to you. It was also very solemn and focused on our reflecting of our sins rather than celebrating the removal of sin and being forgiven 'once and for all' through the cross of Christ, who no longer remembers them. The early church did not see this as a sacrament, but a family meal called 'the love feast' and all were welcome at the table, including the children, and it was a celebrating of the finished work of Christ. It was a communal meal that was very festive and celebratory and was patterned after the Passover meal, which is when Jesus gave the 'last supper' to the disciples.

When Paul is telling the Corinthians in 1 Cor. 11:27-33 to not take it 'unworthily' he is speaking to the wealthy Corinthian believers, who were not waiting for the poor believers to eat with them. They were eating all the food, drinking all the wine and getting drunk before they got there. This is the context of 'examine yourself' or 'check your attitude' of not discerning the body and how you are treating your brothers and sisters by not including them in the meal. Plus, Jesus ended the supper with washing the feet of the least of these, and when we are not serving and loving our brothers and sisters we need to examine our attitudes.

The love feast is NOT about looking for your sin but rejoicing of how God was in Christ reconciling you to Himself; not counting your sins against you, and that is something to dance and celebrate about, not be afraid of. It became more of a Sacrament after the 2nd century when they separated the bread and cup from the meal and made it only something that certain individuals (bishops and priests) could administer. There is nothing wrong with it being a Sacrament but don't make others do it the way you do, because for some it is celebratory and for some it is solemn; just know that its original purpose was a fellowship meal and celebration so, it was NOT always a Sacrament, which is the point of this myth.

Myth #43
When we minister, it is all of Him and none of me.

During my second year of traveling and preaching, I was standing in front of a congregation, after I had just read a Scripture and prayed a prayer that I had heard many pray before, "Tonight, in this service God, let it be all of you and none of me." The moment I prayed this, the Holy Spirit whispered in my heart, *"Well I guess nothing is getting said or done tonight."* I was so shocked, I had my wife sing another song as I had to sit down for a moment while God began to show me how we are co-laborers on the Earth with Him. It is not all of Him and none of me for we are in union, and He has not just given me life, or replaced my life, but Christ is my life. Scripture tells us that without Him we can do nothing; John 15:5, *I am the vine, you are the branches. He who abides in me, and I in him, he bears much fruit, for apart from me you can do nothing;* but with Him we can do all things; Philippians 4:13, *I can do all things through him who strengthens me.*

So, without Him, we cannot but without us, He normally will not. There are a few examples of God intervening in situations of people's lives without human assistance, but those are the exceptions and not the norm. Jesus is our main example of God and man working in tandem and unity. He chooses to speak through us, love through us, heal through us, and produce His life to others through us. Jesus was all God and all man when He was on the Earth and He said, "I only do what I see my Father do, and I only say that which I hear my Father say." He and the Father were one and He prayed that for us in John 17, so we would know that same union of relationship. Theology calls it the 'hypostatic union' which simply means that we are as Jesus is, God-men, or men with divinity living inside.

Jesus would have probably prayed that prayer like this, "Tonight Father, it is all of you and all of me as we minister together to bring life to those around us." In Acts 3, Peter and John come to the temple gate, 'Beautiful' and a man is begging, asking for money, and Peter looks at him and says, *Look on us.* What a bold statement. Notice Peter did not say, 'Don't look at me', I am just a man and will let you down, so only look to God. Instead, he has the boldness to know that what he Had or who he had inside of him is what the man really needed, then he and God ministered healing to that man. Jesus called the Holy Spirit our paraclete or helper; notice, He is not called the 'doer' but the 'helper' in other words, we do it, but He helps and empowers us. So just know that God chooses to use us to manifest His purpose on the Earth and we obviously need Him, but He also chooses to use us, and it is not all of Him and none of me.

Myth #44
There is a perfect and a permissive will of God.

When I was growing up, the message of the perfect will of God tended to scare me some. It seemed like if you really submitted your life to God, He would make you do something you didn't enjoy, or make you live somewhere you hated. He would tell you to do something like, "Go to Africa and minister to Pygmy's" lol, which is what I remember a missionary telling us; or if you made one wrong choice, your life would be off track and forever ruined. I have heard many teachings on the perfect will of God which is mentioned only in Romans 12:2, and the word 'perfect' is translated 'telos' (mature, full grown, developed, complete, and the root of where we get 'it is finished'). Notice, it is different then something you step in and out of, it's something that you mature and grow into and it is also good, well pleasing, and acceptable.

This is speaking of ONE will in 3 stages of growth or maturity. God does not have a plan 'B' period. The Scriptures say absolutely NOTHING about a 'permissive will' and what we would view as permissive is instead just someone walking out God's will in different stages of their life and development through obedience and disobedience. As a matter of fact, there are only a few times in Scripture where the phrase, 'this is the will of God' is used, and none of them have to do with where you live, what you do for a living or who you marry but 'how' you live and the 'attitudes' in which you walk His will or purpose out.

There are many that have the phrase, 'God's will or will of God' but even then, it's more about our walk and obedience then our vocation. A few are Romans 12:1-2, *Therefore I urge you, brethren, by the mercies of God, to present your bodies a living and holy sacrifice, acceptable to God, which is your spiritual service of worship. And do not be conformed to this world, but be transformed by the renewing of your mind, so that you may prove what the will of God is, that which is good and acceptable and perfect.* As well as 1 Thessalonians 5:16-18, *Rejoice always; pray without ceasing; in everything give thanks; for this is God's will for you in Christ, Jesus.* Also, I Thessalonians 4:3-5, *For THIS is the will of God, even your sanctification, that you should abstain from fornication.* Then, 1 Peter 2:15, *For this is the will of God, our sanctification; that is, that you abstain from sexual immorality; that each of you know how to possess his own vessel in sanctification and honor, not in lustful passion, like the Gentiles who do not know God.*

Now this subject is so vast, and many view these things differently, but I believe that we are in His will by believing and being in Christ, and we are on the way to His perfect (mature, complete, and full grown) will as He leads us in our daily lives and we are transformed by the renewing of our minds. The will of God is unfolded in daily reasonable (common sense) service and it is a process of God working out His good pleasure in and through us, which is why we work out our salvation and not work it in. The will of God is not some hyper-spiritual, mystical, floating around 'I just can't seem to find it' kind of thing. Instead, it is a very practical way of living in the Kingdom and simply being led by His Spirit in your day to day life of serving. My point is, there is NOT one Scripture that says anything about a 'permissive will' of God, only THE will of God that is good, acceptable, and perfect (complete). Relax and let God work in you and stop sweating and thinking that every wrong choice is going to lead to you being out of His will, for He will even cause those things to work together for your good because He loves you.

Myth #45
People have always dressed up for church (corporate assembly).

I have had so many people tell me that they would attend church, but they had no 'church clothes.' Now let me start off by saying that whether you like to dress up or dress down for church is completely a preference issue and NOT a spiritual one, and we will find that it is more of a cultural thing than a Scriptural one. So just make sure you don't judge or look down on anyone for whatever they prefer. Some people believe and will nearly fight you over the idea that we should wear our best when coming into God's presence and if you don't, then it's nearly sacrilegious. The problem is, this way of thinking causes people to step into 'dualism' which brings division between the secular and the sacred and the idea that we are not in continual unbroken union with Him no matter where we are. To believe the building we meet in is where we meet with Him, is an Old Covenant mindset and not the New, that shows us we are always in His presence, because His presence is in us, for we are the temple of the Holy Spirit.

Historically, people only started dressing up for services in the mid 1800's or so because before the industrial revolution there was no middle class. People who were not rich only had 2 sets of clothes; one for work and one for town (which were just a little less tattered). Dressing up was only for the wealthy. In some countries, it was actually forbidden for the poor to dress in the garb of the wealthy. Many protestant movements taught against dressing up, like the Methodists who were known for turning someone away from their service for dressing too nice. Also, the early Baptists taught against dressing up because it brought a division between the rich and the poor. The early church also taught the same because they were in a culture that was all about your status and place in society and the gospel made every man equal which was a revolutionary idea. Paul even rebukes the wealthy Corinthian believers for showing up early (because they could) to the love feast or service and drinking all the wine and eating all the food before the poor could get there. The Apostle, James, also rebukes the believers who were treating the rich saints better than the poor (favoritism) and for dressing differently from the poor. Even the preachers in the early church dressed like everyone else and early fathers, like Tertullian and Clement taught that the ministers should be mainly in white apparel which was a heavy influence by Plato who taught that 'white was the color of the gods'.

However, all of that changed after Constantine, who had the 'clergy' dress in Greco-Roman attire with special vestments. Many Bishops then began teaching that the clergy should never enter the Sanctuary in everyday attire. By the 7th &

8th century the church began to teach that all the robes and vestments were inherited from the Levitical priests, in which they were just trying to justify the practice with no Biblical backing and made the clergy dress one way and the 'laity' another, differentiating between the pulpit and the pew. This all changed in the mid 1800's when a Congregational minister named Horace Bushnell wrote an essay called, 'Taste and Fashion' where he argued that Christians should love refinement and that they were attributes of God. Also, another preacher, William Foote, who was Presbyterian wrote an article called, 'Church-going people are a dress loving people'. These articles, along with the rising Victorian culture, took over the church and it became an event to go to, rather than a worship to experience. This changed the way the church functioned from then almost till now.

This subject is all about preference, so whatever you prefer is what you should do, but do not think that someone who does the opposite is religious or sacrilegious. There is no Scripture that tells us how to dress in the New Covenant other than be modest, and for God's sake put on some clothes lol.

*(credit to Frank Viola's book 'Pagan Christianity)

Myth #46
Christians have a heart problem and need to get their heart right with God.

Many of us have been in services where the preacher, near the close, ends with telling believers that their hearts have become cold thru sin and they need to repent and get their heart right with God. I also hear leaders say quite often things like, "They have a heart problem." or "They need a heart check." Now I understand what they mean most of the time, but the verbiage used is not correct for a New Covenant son of God. Also, our English versions use the word 'heart' but in both Old and New Testaments, it is nearly always translated for the soul, Greek (psuche) Hebrew (nephesh). The truth is, we become righteous in our spirits or hearts when we believe and are now the righteousness of God in Christ Jesus, 2 Cor. 5:21, *He made Him who knew no sin to be sin on our behalf, so that we might become the righteousness of God in Him.* We cannot get any more righteous or right with God than we already are. The Kingdom of God and the Godhead take up residence in your spirit and make it whole and complete, and you are then told to work OUT your salvation, not work IN, or work FOR your salvation, because it is something that manifests from the inside out.

What should be said is, repentance (change of mind) gets your soul aligned with your heart (spirit) and the Holy Spirit, who dwells in your spirit. Also, when we receive the Word, He pierces the division of soul (psuche) and spirit (pneuma) and discerns the thoughts and the intents of the heart (kardias-inner man, spirit) Hebrews 4:12, *For the word of God is living and active and sharper than any two-edged sword and piercing as far as the division of soul and spirit, of both joints and marrow, and able to judge the thoughts and intentions of the heart.* When we receive Christ by faith, we get a new and clean heart; a heart completely new, cleansed, and righteous. However, we do not get a new soul (mind, will, and emotions) this is why we are told to renew our minds, put on the mind of Christ, be renewed in the spirit of our minds, have your conscience cleansed etc.

    The struggle for the believer is a fight of faith (trust, belief, confidence) that is waged in our soul and mainly between our ears. 2 Cor. 2:11 says, *so that no advantage would be taken of us by Satan, for we are not ignorant of his schemes (tricks, mind games).* All he has is mind games because he cannot pervert your regenerated spirit. Also 1 Peter 1:9, *Obtaining as the outcome of your faith the salvation of your souls.* So, the soul being saved is the goal or the end result of your faith, not the beginning. When we 'get saved' our spirit is saved, our soul is being saved, and our bodies will be saved. So, do not let anyone tell you that your heart or spirit is not right, but know that we can be saved and still have grave clothes that need to be taken off like Lazarus, and we need our stinking thinking, bad attitudes, and our souls cleansed and transformed.

Myth #47
Your gift 'making room for you' is talking about your spiritual gift opening doors for ministry.

Many of us have heard many leaders say that your gift will make room for you, and most use it in the context of 'if you are wanting God to use you or you have a dream about something then, if you have a gift it will open the right doors for you at the right time.' This also insinuates that if doors are not opening, you must not have a gift or there's something wrong with you. This phrase seems to nearly always get used out of its original context, which has nothing to do with spiritual gifts, and everything to do with giving an actual gift or present to someone that then gives you access to them.

The verse that is used is found in Proverbs 18:16, *A man's gift opens doors for him, and brings him before great men.* It means; gifts, presents, and offerings. It is not talking about spiritual gifts, but literally bringing a gift or an offering to great men. That is what gives you access. Also Proverbs 19:6, *Many seek the favor of the generous man, and everyone is a friend to a giver of gifts.* The word 'gifts' here is the same Hebrew word found in Proverbs 18:16, *A man's gift makes room for him and brings him before great men;* which in its context, is obviously talking about presents and generosity and not a spiritual gift.

In Ancient cultures, including Hebrew culture, if you were going to come into the presence of royalty or a great individual, then you would bring a gift to them. A great example is the Queen of Sheba coming to King Solomon and bringing him many gifts, and he then gave the queen her heart's desire. Also, there are many examples in Scripture of individuals coming into the presence of prophets needing a word from the Lord, bringing a gift or an offering; let alone the Israelites, in the Old Covenant they were told not to come before God empty handed or come into His presence without a gift or an offering. Now even though we have taken this out of its context, can it also be used to mean spiritual gifts? Perhaps, and it probably does not hurt anything, but the fact remains that it is talking about how being a generous gift giver opens hearts and gives access into someone's life.

So, if your boss is constantly irritating you, rather than complain, why don't you get him/her a card telling them that you know how much pressure they must be under and give them a gift card for coffee or a meal, because no one turns down a gift. You never know, it might change their attitude toward you and give you favor with them. I have encouraged young men and women for years that if there is someone you respect and want to emulate, ask if you can take them to lunch and pay for it and watch how they respond. I have done this for years and have consistently watched how gifts have given me favor and access.

Myth #48
When one sinner repents or gets saved all the angels in Heaven rejoice.

The above statement gets declared quite often in church services and rarely does it get questioned, but is that what the Scriptures actually say? The passage that is used is Luke 15:7 & 10, Vs. 7 says, *I tell you, in just the same way there will be more joy in heaven over one sinner who repents than over ninety-nine righteous people who have no need of repentance.* It is an assumption to think that this means the angels are also rejoicing because Vs.10 says, *In the same way, I tell you, there is joy in the presence of the angels of God over one sinner who repents.*

The context of Luke 15 also shows us that it is the one who finds the lost ones who is rejoicing, which culminates in the Father throwing a party for His lost son who returned home.

The Apostle, Peter, tells us in 1 Peter 1:10-12, *As to this salvation, the prophets wo prophesied of the grace that would come to you made careful searches and inquiries, seeking to know what person or time the Spirit of Christ within them was indicating as He predicted the sufferings of Christ and the glories to follow. It was revealed to them that they were not serving themselves, but you, in these things which now have been announced to you through those who preached the gospel to you by the Holy Spirit sent from heaven-things into which angels long to look.* This passage tells us that angels desire to understand salvation because they do not receive salvation, only those who have been born of water and spirit. John 3:3, *Jesus answered and said to him, 'Truly, truly, I say to you, unless one is born-again he cannot see the kingdom of God.'*

This is speaking of natural human birth and then spiritual birth. Angels do not know what it means to be saved, so they long to understand it, and Jesus said in Matthew 24:36, *But of that day and hour no one knows, not even the angels of heaven, nor the son, but the Father alone.*

So, angels are messengers that are not all knowing and because they do not understand the mystery of redemption, they may not be the ones rejoicing. Instead, just maybe it is the God-head rejoicing and the saints, especially after the Resurrection, along with the 'cloud of witness'. We are told in Zephaniah 3:17, *The Lord your God in your midst a victorious warrior. He will exult over you with joy,* (Hebrew; to go around, rejoice and twirl*) HE will be quiet in His love, He will rejoice over you with shouts of joy* (rejoicing because of salvation). This passage shows us that it is God who is rejoicing and not necessarily the angels. Now could angels be rejoicing because they see God doing it? Perhaps, but we do not have Scripture showing that (which is the point of this myth) which shows us that the rejoicing is in the PRESENCE of the angels.

Myth #49
The lion will lay down with the lamb.

If I were to ask most of you to fill in the blank of this statement; the _____ will lay down with the lamb? Most of us would probably say the 'lion' because we have either heard it said or we have said it ourselves, assuming there is a Scripture for it. The only verse that has this verbiage is found in Isaiah 11:6, *The wolf will dwell with the lamb, and the leopard will lie down with the young goat, and the calf and the young lion and the fatling together; and a little boy will lead them.* This whole chapter is speaking of the 'root' of Jesse and pointing to the lineage of David and to Jesus the Messiah; it is showing what the New Covenant will produce in our lives, in this beautiful metaphor. It also shows us what this World will look like when, *the earth will be full of the knowledge of the Lord as the waters cover the sea.* V:9. It is our job to declare the gospel which is that 'knowledge'. The real message, once this Messiah comes, is how He will bring a Kingdom of peace to such a degree that former enemies will be at peace with each other and stop killing one another.

Isaiah 65:25, *The wolf and the lamb shall graze together; the lion shall eat* straw *like the ox, and dust shall be the serpent's food. They will do no evil or harm in all My holy mountain, says the Lord.* This is an awesome picture of former enemies;

Jew's and Gentiles, now becoming one in Christ. This becomes a reality every time a Jew and an Arab meet Christ and choose to work together and not fight. Also, every time we choose to love our enemies and release the peace of the Kingdom, it is a manifestation of the government of God which is one of peace, not war, death or violence.

Now is there anything necessarily wrong with the saying since lions are in the same verse, and perhaps lions will also lie down with the lambs? I would say that it is nothing to argue about, but the wolf and the lamb is a more powerful metaphor, since the wolf is nearly always a picture of our enemies, and lions at times, as Jesus and those fighting for us. So, since the Kingdom is at hand, in and among us, let us live in the same manner as Paul tells us; try and live peaceably with all men.

Myth #50
Principalities and powers are demons and only speaking of demonic hierarchies.

I grew up in the Pentecostal/Charismatic stream of the body of Christ, and anytime someone talked about principalities and powers, we immediately went to visions of the book, 'This Present Darkness' where there were all different levels of demons in this incredibly organized army of the devil. We of course ignored the idea of him being a liar, the author of confusion and not the smartest entity, but I digress, lol. I sat in a Saturday seminar in the 90's, as we were taught there were General demons and Captain demons and Sergeant demons and then the regular ones were just imps and foot soldiers. What I find interesting is that we are told by the Apostle Paul in Titus 3:1, *Remind the people to be subject to rulers, to authorities, to be obedient, to be ready for every good deed* (NASB), while the KJV says to be subject to principalities and powers. These phrases are the same Greek words 'Arche' and 'Exousia'. The form and figure of speech in each context is also found in Ephesians 1:21, *Far above all rule and authority and power and dominion, and every name that is named, not only in this age but also in the one to come.* Eph 6:12, *For our struggle is not against flesh and blood, but*

against the rulers, against the powers, against the world forces of this darkness, against the spiritual forces of wickedness in the heavenly places. Then Eph. 3:10, *So that the manifold wisdom of God might now be made known through the church to the rulers and the authorities in the heavenly places.*
1 Corinthians 15:24, Romans 8:38, as well as Colossians 1:16, *For in Him all things were created, things in Heaven and on Earth, visible and invisible, whether thrones or dominions or rulers or authorities, all things were created through Him and for Him.*

    These few passages are NOT all talking about demonic authorities but also human ones that rule the systems of this World. We are told in 1 Corinthians 2:8, *"The wisdom which none of the rulers of this age has understood; for if they had understood it they would not have crucified the Lord of glory;* This is definitely NOT talking about demons because they knew who Jesus was. Also, in Acts 19:15, *And the evil spirit answered and said to them, "I recognize Jesus, and I know about Paul, but who are you?"* When Jesus would show up to cast out demons they would say, *"Have you come to torment us before our time, Son of God?"* Matthew 8:*29 And they cried out saying, "What business do we have with each other, Son of God? Have You come to torment us before the time?"* Then, Mark 1:24, *Saying, "What business do we have with each other, Jesus of Nazareth? Have You come to destroy us? I know who You are, the Holy One of God!"*

We know that it was Pilate, Herod, and Caiaphas the high priest, as well as the Jewish temple system that crucified the Lord and not demons. These three rulers represented the empires of that age, one was the political, another the commerce, and the last the religious. If they would have known who He was they would not have crucified Him but received Him as their Messiah

I believe that all principalities and powers and rulers can be demonically influenced, but it is bad exegesis to say, when you see these words, it is talking about demon powers. Many times, depending on the context it's talking about, human magistrates and rulers in high and lofty positions of authority or at times, the law system that was being done away with in Christ. Now are there demons? Yes, and do they influence mankind? Yes, they can, but just know they have been defeated and stripped of any power or authority, now all they can do is deceive men with lies and imaginations that become strongholds of thinking. The sad thing is that much of the church puts such focus on them, they end up re- empowering dis- empowered spirits.

It is also bad exegesis to say there are no more principalities, powers and rulers because I can go to my local branch of government downtown and it is called a principality, so the systems are still around and that's what Paul was saying to obey. That's why we do not wrestle with the men but the systems of thought that rule them and drive our nations and World.

Myth #51

Shadrach, Meshach and Abednego said to the king, "Our God will deliver us, but even if HE doesn't we are not bowing our knee to your idols.

For years, I have heard preachers say, "God is able to deliver you, but even if He doesn't we are going to be like the three Hebrew boys and still not bow our knee to the devil or this world." It sounds spiritual by saying, "Even if He doesn't I am still going to serve Him." but is this really what they were saying? When we read Scripture in context, it changes so many of our preconceived ideas about a passage. Many of us have heard things said in certain ways for so long we just accept that it means what we heard. We can also get mixed up because most translations put their doctrinal bias in with the actual translating of the original text which is why we study to show ourselves approved and not just read. This comes from the book of Daniel 3:17-18, *If that be so, our God who we serve is able to deliver us from the furnace of blazing fire; and He will deliver us out of your hand oh King. But even if He does not, let it be known to you, oh King, that we are not going to serve your Gods, or worship the golden image you have set up.* (NASB). When we read this version, which I normally prefer, but in this instance the translators of the NASB have added their bias and belief in to the text just like the NIV and a few others. If you go to the original text and check out the literal translations such as, the Youngs Literal Translation (YLT) they agree more with the KJV & NKJV on this one. You can even do something as simple as biblehub.com then put the passage in and click on Hebrew and it will show you that the *'even if He doesn't'* is not there, it simply just says, "but if not".

    What we are saying here is, we must first go to the context; the King tells the people that when you hear the music play you are to bow your knee or get thrown in to the fire. So, the whole point is whether you get thrown into the fire or not, and not whether God delivers you or doesn't. The three young men then say to the King, "If that be so." If what be so? IF YOU THROW US INTO THE FIRE, then our God is able to deliver us, and He will deliver us from your hand. They boldly confess twice that God can and will deliver them. In other words, there is no double mindedness going on at all as they are confident and full of faith. They then say, "But if not." If not what? IF YOU DON'T THROW US INTO THE FIRE, not if God doesn't deliver us. If you are thrown into a fire you will have no knee to bow on or have anything to serve anyway, because you will be dead, lol.

This whole story has no "but if He doesn't" connected to it at all. It is a testimony to the faithfulness of God towards young men of faith who boldly stand for what they believe. This mistranslation can lead many to have a 'but if God doesn't' mentality, when that is not what it means. Now let me also say that God is not a genie in the bottle either and there is a reality of 'Even if He doesn't do what I asked or want' I will still love and serve Him, but this passage is not saying that at all.

Myth #52
Michael, Gabriel, and Lucifer were all called archangels in the Scriptures.

This one is interesting to me because many of the things that we tend to divide and disagree over are not real clear in Scripture, and some of these things we may never know on this side of the seen world. There may be thousands of archangels in Heaven, but we only have what is recorded in Scripture, as well as a few historical books that some embrace as also inspired; and yet some in Christianity refute them. First, the ONLY two times the word archangel is used is Jude 9, *Michael, the archangel* in which the word, 'archangel' is not plural and denotes a singular chief ranking angel. Also, I Thessalonians 4:16, *The Lord will descend from Heaven with the voice of the archangel.* But that one does not name anyone; it just says the voice of. So, according to Scripture, there is only one recorded archangel named, Michael.

Now, throughout church history, many early church fathers as well as some denominations teach and embrace that there are seven archangels which they get from the Apocryphal books that some have in their Bibles. These seven were Michael, Gabriel, Raphael, Uriel, Cyril, Ramiel, and Raguel. These come from the books of Enoch, as well as Tobit, and II Esdras, and are still embraced as inspired by some Christian denominations. Gabriel is called a messenger in Scripture, Daniel 8:16, *And I heard the voice of a man between the banks of Ulai, and he called out and said, "Gabriel, give this man an understanding of the vision."* Daniel 9:21, *While I was still speaking in prayer, then the man Gabriel, whom I had seen in the vision previously, came to me in my extreme weariness about the time of the evening offering.* And Luke 1:19, *The angel answered and said to him, "I am Gabriel, who stands in the presence of God, and I have been sent to speak to you and to bring you this good news."* He was never called an archangel, and Lucifer was NOT an angel at all, or even a name (for more on that look at myth #1). We do not really know if there are 1, 7, or 700 and can only decide by faith what we believe from the Scriptures; which is the point of this book, to expose Myths and Mistranslations in the Bible.

Myth #53
When you get saved your name is written in the Lambs book of life.

I grew up hearing evangelists and pastors after an altar call, where people had said the 'Sinners prayer' (an earlier myth) make the statement, "Now that you received Christ, your name has been written in the Lambs book of life." In other words, now you are in and God has written your name on the Heavenly roll; so, when the roll is called up yonder, I will be there, lol (old hymn humor). The problem comes in when you try to support it with actual Scripture. I was first challenged to look at this differently in 1993, when my spiritual mother, Dr. Fuchsia Pickett, in one of her messages, said it wasn't in the Bible. So afterwards, while we were eating, I questioned her because it went against everything I had been taught. She challenged me to go look up the supporting Scriptures and bring them to lunch the next day. I took the challenge, went home and studied to prove her wrong. Well, she was right, and I was wrong, and I have been on a 28-year journey of being wrong quite a bit, but at least admitting it.

So, where we get this from is Revelation 3:5-6, *He who overcomes will thus be clothed in white garment; and I will not erase his name from the book of life, and I will confess his name before My Father and before His angels. He who has an ear, let him hear what the Spirit says to the churches.* Also, Revelation 20:15, *Anyone who was found whose name was not written in the book of life, he was thrown into the lake of fire.* Then Revelation 13:8, *All who dwell on the earth will worship him, everyone whose name has not been written from the foundation of the world in the book of life of the Lamb who has been slain.* As well as Revelation 17:8, *The beast that you saw was, and is not, and is about to come up out of the abyss and go to destruction. And those who dwell on the earth, whose name has not been written in the book of life from the foundation of the world, will wonder when they see the beast, that he was and is not and will come;* Psalm 69:28, *May they be blotted out of the book of life and may they not be recorded with the righteous.* Then in Exodus 32:33, *The LORD said to Moses, "Whoever has sinned against Me, I will blot him out of My book.*

    These all speak about names being blotted out, but when they are put in seems to imply before the foundation of the World. Then you have Luke 10:20, *Do not rejoice that spirits are subject to you but rejoice that your names are written in Heaven.* So, the question, if this is a salvation issue, when did their names get written in Heaven? The lamb was still with them and had not died yet. Revelation 13:8 (NASB), *All who dwell on the Earth will worship him--everyone whose names have not been written from the foundation of the World in the book of life of the Lamb who has been slain.* This seems to say that names are written from the foundation of the World, so that throws a monkey wrench in the whole thing. Eph. 1:4 also tells us that He chose us in Him before the foundation of the world; *Just as He chose us in Him before the foundation of the world, that we would be holy and blameless before Him. In love.*

So, my friends, praying a prayer does not put your name necessarily in, but we are told that names can be blotted out, and the meaning of those passages can be argued in a few different directions, because they are apocalyptic language.

Myth #54
Jesus kept the law of Moses perfectly to fulfill it!

Jesus said in Matthew 5:17, *Do not think that I have come to abolish the law or the prophets; I did not come to abolish but fulfill* (complete or finish by bringing to an end) NASB. Fulfilling the law and prophets did not mean keeping the law perfectly. Jesus not only broke the law quite a bit, but even rebuked and reinterpreted it. In the Sermon on the Mount, He says over and over, *You have heard said, but I now say unto you* (the things that they had heard were from the law of Moses). We are told in Romans 13:10, *Love is the fulfillment of the law*. Jesus, who is love, fulfilled the law not by keeping it, but by showing what the law of God looks like, which is love. Jesus ate when He shouldn't have, He touched what He shouldn't have, He was friends with who He wasn't supposed to be friends with, and He broke the law of Moses often, but He never broke the law of God, which is love.

Every time Jesus broke the law, it was for love and to show that it was man that wanted the Mosaic covenant and not Him. We are told in Psalms 40:6, *Sacrifice and meal offerings You have not desired; my ears you have opened; burnt offering and sin offering you have not required.* Also, in Jeremiah 7:22-23, *For I did not speak to your fathers, or command them in the day that I brought them out of the land of Egypt, concerning burnt offerings and sacrifices. But this is what I commanded them, saying, 'Obey my voice, and I will be your God and you will be my people; and you will walk in all the way which I command you, that it may be well with you.'* The next verse goes on to say, *'But they did not obey my voice'*. So, God says through David and Jeremiah that He never told them to do much of what the law commanded, but His desire was that they obey His voice.

Jesus kept the Law of God perfectly, but broke the law of Moses often, showing us that the Royal law (James 2:8) is to love humanity, for love never fails, and love is the fulfillment of the law. Jesus' life showed us what God really looks like and revealed what God views as law compared to Moses and men. Romans 10:4, *But Christ is the end of the law for righteousness to everyone who believes.* The only law we now keep is the Royal law of life, love, and liberty in Christ Jesus. Jesus has now brought the law to a telos (end) so we are NOT empowered by grace to keep the law of

Moses, but we are empowered to keep the law of God, which is love.

Myth #55
Heaven and Earth will literally pass away.

Many of us were raised believing this because it literally says this in the Bible and Jesus was the one who said it. First, in Matthew 24:35, *Heaven and Earth will pass away, but My words shall not pass away,* and Matthew 5:18, *Until Heaven and Earth pass away, not the smallest letter or stroke shall pass from the Law until all is accomplished.* The problem is, we are reading a 1st century book with 21st century lenses most of the time, and we do not understand apocalyptic language, which is full of hyperbole and metaphors and rarely literal. We also must put ourselves into the minds of 1st century 2nd temple Jews who were the audience that Jesus was talking to.

The question should be, "Why would Heaven ever need to pass away since that is a perfect place of God's manifest presence?" Plus, we are told several times, in the Old Testament, like Psalm 104:5, *He established the earth upon its foundations, so that it will not totter forever and ever.* Ecclesiastes 1:4, *A generation goes, and a generation comes, but the earth remains forever.* We should also ask if Heaven and Earth didn't pass away, then are we still under the law and should we throw out most of the epistles, which tell us we are not? Lastly, what is, *'till all fulfilled'* talking about? The law fulfilled? We know that Christ in His finished work fulfilled the law and the prophets, right? To understand what Jesus meant, we must realize, to a first century Jew, Heaven and Earth were the Temple and its system, Heaven and Earth, Isaiah 51:15-16, *For I am the LORD your God, who stirs up the sea and its waves roar (the LORD of hosts is His name). I have put My words in your mouth and have covered you with the shadow of My hand, to establish the heavens, to found the earth, and to say to Zion, 'You are My people.*

Haggai 2:21-22, *Speak to Zerubbabel governor of Judah, saying, "I am going to shake the heavens and the earth. I will overthrow the thrones of kingdoms and destroy the power of the kingdoms of the nations; and I will overthrow the chariots and their riders, and the horses and their riders will go down, everyone by the sword of another."* Deuteronomy 32:1, *Give ear, O heavens, and let me speak; and let the earth hear the words of my mouth;* Just to name few.

Josephus, a Jewish historian, hired by the Romans to take meticulous records of the war from 67-70 A.D. says in his writing, 'Antiquities of the Jews' (Book 3, Chapter 7)

"When Moses distinguished the Tabernacle into 3 parts, and allowed 2 of them for the priests; as a place accessible and common, he denoted the land and seas; these being of general access to all, but he set apart the third division for God, because Heaven is inaccessible to men." Second Temple Jews called The Outer Court; The Sea. The Inner Court; The Earth. And the Holy of Holies; The Heavens--where God dwells.

So to a 1st Century Jew, when their Temple and Holy City was destroyed in 70 A.D, THEIR Heaven and THEIR Earth did pass away, by fire no less, and the elements (rudiments) in the temple were destroyed and melted like wax, 2 Peter 3:10, *But the day of the Lord will come like a thief, in which the heavens will pass away with a roar and the elements will be destroyed with intense heat, and the earth and its works will be burned up.*

This fulfilled the law and the prophets, for there was now no longer a place where they could offer sacrifices; and the law, which the cross had made obsolete, had now completely passed away, Hebrews 8:13, *When He said, 'A new covenant' He has made the first obsolete. But whatever is becoming obsolete and growing old is ready to disappear.* We are then told in Revelation

21:1, *Then I saw a new heaven and a new earth; for the first heaven and the first earth passed away, and there is no longer any sea.* Their Temple had been completely destroyed and now there is a new Heaven and new Earth, which is the Temple not made with hands or straw, or mortar and bricks; but made by God.

No wonder Paul has to say it twice when he says, "Know ye not, know ye not, you are THE TEMPLE." I would encourage all of you to study this out more and realize that there are more than 300 figures of speech in the Scriptures, and the Hebrew language was full of idioms, hyperbole, metaphor, similes, and apocalyptic and parabolic language, which is NOT literal. So just know that literal Heaven and Earth are NOT going anywhere, and the law has been completely fulfilled. The only Temple God desires to live in is the Tabernacle among men, which is our bodies.

Myth #56
In Acts 19 Paul is asking a group of Christians if they have received the Holy Spirit since they have believed.

I grew up in the Pentecostal world which gave me wonderful experiences and passions, but also horrible exegeses and ways of interpreting Scripture. I remember my 'go to' verse when speaking with non-Pentecostals about the Holy Spirit; I would tell them, "You are saved but you need to 'get' the Holy Ghost." lol. That type of thinking produces nothing but arrogance and a mindset of "I'm more spiritual than you." The whole passage gives us another view, and in context has nothing to do with what I heard preached most of my life.

In Acts 19:2-5, *Paul asks some disciples, 'Did you receive Holy Spirit when you believed?' 'No, we have not even heard whether there is a Holy Spirit.' And he said, 'Into what then were you baptized? And they said, 'Into John's baptism.' Paul said, 'John's baptized with the baptism of repentance. telling the people to believe in Him who was coming after him, that is, in Jesus. When they heard this, they were baptized into the name of The Lord Jesus.* He told the people to believe in the One coming after him, that is, in Jesus. *When they heard this, they were baptized into the name of The Lord Jesus. And when Paul laid hands on them, the Holy Spirit came upon them, and they spoke in tongues and prophesied.*

We cannot be 'saved' without the Holy Spirit; Rom. 8:9, *However you are not in the flesh but in the Spirit, if indeed the Spirit of God dwells in you. But if anyone does not have the Spirit of Christ, he does not belong to Him.* He draws us, inhabits us, and illuminates us to the Gospel and to the reality of our reconciliation with the Father. To tell someone they are saved, but do not have the Holy Spirit is 'Ignorance of Scripture 101' especially since Jesus said, *Out of your innermost being will flow rivers of living water.* Speaking of the Holy Spirit, who had not yet been poured out (John 7:38-39).

Notice, He did not say, "After you believe, God is going to drop a river (Holy Spirit) on you from the sky." The Holy Spirit comes from within. The Holy Spirit is already there; just as Jesus breathed on them and they received the Holy Spirit in the new birth; (salvation John 20) then on the day of Pentecost He flowed out of them.

This passage in Acts 19, in context, makes it very clear that they had received a message of repentance from dead works and religion (Johns') but not yet heard of Jesus, so they had not heard the Gospel yet. So, Paul preaches it to them and then baptizes them in the name of Jesus and then the Holy Spirit in them comes flowing out of them, manifesting in tongues and prophecy, thru the laying on of hands. They were not 'Christians' yet and had not believed in Jesus. So, the myth of this passage is that Paul asked a group of Christians if they had received the Holy Spirit, which is not true because they were not. I have heard famous Pentecostal preachers teach that Ephesus was a Baptist church and Paul turned them into a Pentecostal one, and there was a season I would have shouted them down. lol

Myth #57
He that endures till the end will be saved is talking about salvation and making it in to Heaven.

The statement, 'He that endures till the end will be saved' is found a few times in the gospels. Jesus first says it to His disciples as He tells them He is sending them out as sheep among wolves, and then informs them of how they will be persecuted for His name sake. It is found in Matthew 10:22, *You will be hated by all because of my name, but it is the one who has endured till the end who will be saved* (delivered, preserved). Then in Vs. 23 He says, *but whenever they persecute you in one city, flee to the next; for truly I say to you, you will not finish going through the cities of Israel until the Son of Man comes.*

It doesn't sound like it's the end of their life, but perhaps the end of something else? Also, in Mark 13:13, *You will be hated by all because of My name, but the one who endures to the end, he will be saved.* It's the same as Matthew 24:13, *But the one who endures to the end, he will be saved.* This is in the context of the destruction of the Jewish Temple and Jerusalem, at the end of the age (mistranslated as 'world' in the KJV) which is the Old Covenant age and Jewish sacrificial system.

Jesus is telling them (in context) when the end will be; the tribulation that will occur in their generation and what they must endure to physically survive through it.

Ever since I was young child, I remember preachers, Sunday school teachers and others quote these verses by adding, "You will make it into Heaven if you stay holy, faithful, righteous, and live right all the way to the end of your life." Then many would add, "But if you don't, then He will say, *Depart from me you worker of iniquity, I never knew you*" (Myth #40). The HUGE problem with this thinking is that we are saved by grace, thru faith, and not by our works. Eph. 2:8-9, *For by grace you have been saved through faith, and that not of yourselves, it is the gift of God; not as a result of works, so that no one may boast.*

Righteousness is imputed to us and it is a free gift that cannot be earned, 2 Cor. 5:21, *He made Him who knew no sin to be sin on our behalf, so that we might become the righteousness of God in Him.* Then in Rom. 4:5, *But to the one who does not work, but believes in Him who justifies the ungodly, his faith is credited as righteousness.* So, if my enduring is what gets me into Heaven, then I got myself there by my own efforts. Scripture, in the New Covenant, teaches us the opposite. My works or behavior does not save me or keep me saved; it is believing in Jesus that seals me in Heaven, period.

However, I do believe that an enduring faith, trust, and belief is important in our walk with God. We are not saved by works, but Eph. 2:10 tells us we are saved 'for' good works, as it pertains to our purpose and Kingdom advancement on the Earth, *For we are His workmanship, created in Christ Jesus for good works, which God prepared beforehand so that we would walk in them.* So, endurance and perseverance are good things, but these passages are not about getting into Heaven if we hang on and press thru, which is the point of this myth.

Myth #58

'Work out your salvation with fear and trembling' means to live afraid and in a state of anxiety and nervousness of perhaps losing that salvation.

This passage in Philippians has been used by many to instill fear in people and cause them to work 'for' rather than 'out' their salvation (wholeness, completeness, health, deliverance) and to live afraid of losing out with God and being abandoned or being told to 'depart' (Myth #40) and lose this free gift. I have heard it said, for years, that a text out of context is just a con, and this is a great example of how pulling a verse out of its setting and meaning to its original audience can wreak havoc.

Philippians 2:5-11, *Have this attitude in yourselves which was also in Christ Jesus, who, although He existed in the form of God, did not regard equality with God a thing to be grasped, but emptied Himself, taking the form of a bond-servant, and being made in the likeness of men. Being found in appearance as a man, He humbled Himself by becoming obedient to the point of death, even death on a cross. For this reason, also, God highly exalted Him, and bestowed on Him the name which is above every name, so that at the name of Jesus*

EVERY KNEE WILL BOW, of those who are in heaven and on earth and under the earth, and that every tongue will confess that Jesus Christ is Lord, to the glory of God the Father.

It's all about Christ humbling Himself and taking on the form of humanity, submitting to the death on the cross and the Father, then exalting Him. Then, Vs.12-13, *So then, my beloved, just as you have always obeyed, not as in my presence only, but now much more in my absence, work out your salvation with fear and trembling; for it is God who is at work in you, both to will and to work for His good pleasure.*

The phrase 'fear and trembling' in the first century, was a figure of speech that denoted the opposite of self-confidence or self-righteousness. Another example is when Titus came to the Corinthian church and was encouraged by their reception of him with 'fear and trembling' or with 'respect and awe' with no self-confidence or self-righteousness; because it would make no sense that he would be encouraged, terrified and trembling at the same time, lol. Paul also used this language when coming to the Corinthian church in I Cor. 2:3, *With much weakness, and fear (*awe, reverence*) and much trembling).* Paul was saying, I am not coming in my own strength nor wise and persuasive words but relying wholly on His grace and power in and thru me.

The context of Philippians 2:12-13 ends with Paul telling them that it is GOD who works in us to will and to work for His good pleasure, so stop trying to accomplish this in your own strength and let God do it thru you; *So then, my beloved, just as you have always obeyed, not as in my presence only, but now much more in my absence, work out your salvation with fear and trembling; for it is God who is at work in you, both to will and to work for His good pleasure.* This passage does not promote working 'FOR' our salvation, but instead allowing God to work it out of us, according to His good pleasure, and our work is just to believe and obey.

Isaiah 66:2, *For My hand made all these things, thus all these things came into being, declares the Lord. But to this the one to whom I will look; he who is humble and contrite in spirit and trembles at my word.* Here we have an example of trembling and humility with no self-righteousness in the same text, showing us that our 'doing' this is NOT what this is talking about, but our receiving by grace, thru faith (with a heart of humility) what He has already done in us. Fear, depending upon the context, can be interpreted as terror, but also awe, respect, and reverence. In the New Covenant,

John tells us that perfect love removes all fear (terror) but it does not remove awe and reverence; so just know, my friends, that your Father will in no wise cast you out. So, have faith (trust and confidence) in God and not ourselves, knowing that He who started a good work in us is able to bring it to completion, and He doesn't partly save us, but saves us to the uttermost.

Myth #59
Genesis tells us that Noah preached repentance to his generation before the flood.

I remember actually preaching this in part of a sermon years ago and someone questioned me asking where it actually said that. I went and looked it up and found that nowhere in the Genesis account or the Old Testament is it in the actual Scriptures. I remember thinking, "Then where in the world did I get that from?" You have to actually go to the New Testament and read 2 Peter 2:5, *And did not spare the ancient world, but preserved Noah, a preacher of righteousness, with seven others, when He brought a flood upon the world of the ungodly*

So, Peter tells us that Noah preached righteousness, but it is not recorded anywhere in the Canon of 'what' he preached; it is in other Jewish writings also, as oral traditions were handed down. The Pseudepigrapha (falsely attributed works) book of Sybil, as well as the books of Adam and Eve and the writings of Philo and Josephus share the idea that God was trying to save that generation thru the preaching of Noah. St. Augustine taught that Noah preached for 100 years, yet there is no Scripture to support this.

The Genesis account tells us that God

told him to build for Noah, himself, his family and the animals; no one else. So even if he did preach to them, he was not instructed to according to recorded Scripture. It kind of seems cold of God that He seemed to make up His mind to be done with them without any preaching or grace for Noah's generation. Now do I believe He probably gave more instruction than what is recorded? Yes, if the story of Noah is historical and not myth, as many theologians and early fathers taught, it would make sense to me that He would, but that's not the point of this myth which is, 'Genesis tells us that He did'. Just know, there are many things the Bible records, which have no other Scripture to back it up, but you can find it in extra-Biblical writings. This does not negate them but diffuses the silly argument that I only need to read the Bible to understand the Bible. There is obviously more to read then just the 66 books.

Myth #60
The Bible has always been 66 books.

When it comes to the Bible in Western church culture, you have to be very careful what you say because it has become the 4th person of the Godhead. People fight over their favorite version and claim theirs is THE only right translation and then demonize all others. Yet, most have never studied what the canonization process was like or how much the early fathers, bishops, and theologians struggled with the process. Most just seem to accept that it seemed to mystically appear and God Himself wrote it.

There was no accepted and formalized canonized Bible until the 390's or so, even though it had been put together by the 200's, and even though it was being circulated and received, it was still being discussed and had not yet been recognized formally by the church. Plus, it was 80 books because the early fathers embraced the Apocrypha and the Septuagint (the Greek rendering of the Old Testament that Jesus and the disciples would have been taught from).

The New testament is full of quotes from the Apocryphal books that many have thrown out. As a matter of fact, the 1611 KJV was 80 books and stayed that way until the 1880's, when it was changed to 66 books. I just thought I would add this for all you, the 1611 KJV IS THE WORD OF GOD folks who have been missing 14 inspired books, lol.

Also, during the reformation, Martin Luther started throwing books out that didn't line up with his new found understanding. He got rid of the extra 14 books he didn't agree with in the Old Testament, and tried to get rid of James, Hebrews, Jude, and Revelation in the New, and because the reformers couldn't agree, they left them in.

Those of us in the 21st century seem to assume a lot of things about Scripture, yet when studying history, we realize there has been serious misinformation and fighting over what is inspired and what isn't. If you are Catholic or Orthodox, you embrace what became known as the Apocrypha or the 80 books. If you are a Protestant, you assume we have always had 66 books and the other is just a Catholic thing, and yet many Protestant Bibles were still the 80 up until the 19th century.

The well-known author and theologian, R.C. Sproul is quoted as saying, "The Catholic church believes in an infallible list of infallible books, while the Protestant churches believe in a fallible list of infallible books."

    Just know that above all else, what Jesus came to reveal as God in the flesh is what we are to focus on and know that it's easy to get sidetracked into thinking that none of it is valuable, which is not true. The point of this myth is NOT to discredit the Scriptures, but to show us how they have not always just been 66 books, but for 1500 years there were 80 which were constantly fought about and argued over. Many have struggled in this search for truth and we should be careful when calling something 'false' or 'uninspired' when it just may be. Keep Jesus at the center and you will stay grounded.

Myth #61

What is called the Ten Commandments in the Bible are the ones that many were taught in Sunday school and are in courthouses all over America.

The Ten Commandments are those laws that God had Moses give to the people of Israel as a sign of His Covenant with them while in the wilderness. The 'Big Ten' as some have called it, as well as the law of Moses, and what Paul in the New Testament called, 'The Ministry of Death and Condemnation' written on stones in 2 Cor. 3:7-10, *But if the ministry of death, in letters engraved on stones, came with glory so that the sons of Israel could not look intently at the face of Moses because of the glory of his face, fading as it was, how will the ministry of the Spirit fail to be even more with glory? For if the ministry of condemnation has glory, much more does the ministry of righteousness abound in glory. For indeed what had glory, in this case has no glory because of the glory that surpasses it.*

They are normally called the 'moral laws' also. We get this from Exodus 20, then the same list is also in Deut. 5. However, there is a different list in Exodus 34 and ONLY that one is actually called the 'Ten Commandments' by God. Exodus 34:27-28. *Then the*

LORD said to Moses, "Write down these words, for in accordance with these words, I have made a covenant with you and with Israel." So, he was there with the LORD forty days and forty nights; he did not eat bread or drink water. And he wrote on the tablets the words of the covenant, the Ten Commandments.

Now, the Ten Commandments most of us have heard or were made to memorize, and that which is in courthouses around the U.S.A. is the Exodus 20 list that reads like this:

(KJV)
1. I am Yahweh your God, and you shall have no other gods before me.
2. You shall not make for yourself a statue or any graven image.
3. You shall not take the name of the Lord thy God in vain.
4. Remember the Sabbath day and keep it holy.
5. Honor your father and your mother.
6. Thou shall not kill.
7. Thou shall not commit adultery.
8. Thou shall not steal.
9. Thou shall not bear false witness against your neighbor
10. Thou shall not covet anything that is your neighbors.

However, this list is NOT called, The Ten Commandments by God, even though they were commands He gave. The list in Exodus 34:10-28 is, and they read like this:

(KJV)

1. You shall worship no other god's, for the Lord your God is a jealous God.
2. You shall make thee no molten god's.
3. The feast of unleavened bread thou shall keep.
4. You shall redeem every firstborn of your son's and your flocks.
5. You shall observe the Sabbath and rest after six days of work
6. You shall observe the feast of weeks, first-fruits of the wheat harvest, and the feast of ingathering at the end of the year.
7. Three times a year shall all of your men children appear before the Lord. (also known as Passover, Pentecost, and tabernacles).
8. You shall not offer the blood of my sacrifice with leaven.
9. The first of the first fruits of thy land shall you bring into the house of the Lord thy God.
10. Thou shall not cook a kid goat in its mother's milk.

The first list is what most call THE Ten Commandments; maybe because they are moral and ethical in nature. Yet, the second list is what God called THE Ten Commandments and they don't seem to get the same press, lol; maybe because they are more ritualistic observances, that apply more specifically to Hebrews and not everyone, especially Gentiles. Now, the Good News is that we who live on this side of the cross and are partakers of the New and better Covenant are not under either of these ten, because the finished work of the cross has made them obsolete and they have passed away Heb. 8:13, *When He said, "A new covenant," He has made the first obsolete. But whatever is becoming obsolete and growing old is ready to disappear.*

We are not under law, but grace, thank God. So just know that both of these are in the Bible, but only one is actually called THE TEN COMMANDMENTS!

Myth #62
Non-alcoholic grape juice is always what the church drank at Communion (Eucharist).

 Many of us, raised in Protestant denominations or movements, were taught this, which many believed, and some still do. However, the truth is, grape juice was not even invented, until 1869, by a Methodist minister by the name of Thomas Welch; yup that's where Welch's grape juice comes from. He found a way to use a process to pasteurize the grapes, which would kill the yeast in the grape's (Thomas Bramwell Welch-Wikipedia). He did this because his denomination was in a huge campaign called the Temperance Movement because of so much alcohol abuse. Prohibition was the desire then of many in the church world and they were looking for an alternative to their culture at the time. We also know from New Testament Scriptures like, I Cor.11:20-21, Paul is rebuking some of the church for showing up early to the love feast and family meal (communion) and for eating all the food, before the poor people got there; and some were getting drunk, *Therefore when you meet together, it is not to eat the Lord's Supper, 1 for in your eating each one takes his own supper first; and one is hungry and another is drunk.* Well. there you go. This was NOT happening with grape juice. Paul did a good job of dealing with it and making clear that it was out of order and he later tells the Ephesians, *And, do not be drunk with wine, for this is dissipation, but be inebriated with the Holy Spirit* (Eph. 5:18).

Now, I'm not promoting alcohol consumption; that's a personal choice for each individual, and I'm definitely not promoting drunkenness, which Scripture is pretty clear about. Every person knows their issues, habits, addictions, and limitations. I decided a long time ago to live a Romans 14 life of not being a stumbling block to anyone over what I eat, drink, wear etc. However, the point of this myth is that the church for 1800 years drank wine at the love feast and not grape juice, since it was not even invented yet. So, my friends, that does not mean we have to change the way we do it, but let's just tell people that we are living out Romans 14 and we don't want to stir up anyone's old desires that could lead them to excess, rather than try to twist Scripture to mean something it never did.

Myth #63
If you add to or take away from the Bible, then curses will come upon you.

I have heard people quote this from the time I was a young boy and they got it from Revelation 22:18-1, *I testify to everyone who hears the words of the prophecy of this book: if anyone adds to them, God will add to him the plagues that are written in this book, and if anyone takes away from the words of this book of prophecy, God will take away his part from the tree of life and from the holy city, which are written in this book.*

The problem is with context, because John is not writing about the whole Bible of 66 books or the 80, which were the original Canon, he is specifically talking about the singular book of Revelation. The Bible was not even compiled when this was written, so he could not be speaking about that; plus, the Bible is NOT A book, but a group of books compiled into a single volume that wonderfully harmonizes, in prophetic pictures all pointing to Christ.

John is actually using verbiage from the law of Moses where God told them in Deuteronomy 4:2 & 12:32, not add to or take away from what He *had* commanded them, but to obey His commands, (4:2) *You shall not add to the word which I am commanding you, nor take away from it, that you may keep the commandments of the LORD your God which I command you.* (12:32) *Whatever I command you, you shall be careful to do; you shall not add to nor take away from it.*

The sad thing is, by the time Jesus showed up, the Scribes and Pharisees had done that exact thing and added over 240 more laws and 365 prohibitions. This is why Jesus would say to them, 'you do not even keep the law, and your traditions (or the things they had added) were making the Scriptures of no effect.' Plus, if we believed this referred to the whole Bible then we Protestants, who embrace the 66 book Canon, would have to explain why we took away 14 books, lol.

So, this is NOT speaking about the whole of Scripture, but the book of Revelation specifically. This is why I wrote this book on Myths, because people add to and take away things all the time, that are not even said or meant in Scripture.

Myth #64
The Bible tells believers they should die daily.

    I have heard so many sermons telling me to die daily as they reference Jesus saying, 'to deny ourselves and take up our cross to follow Him.' These two things are not one in the same, because denying oneself is not committing spiritual suicide every day so we can walk in the Spirit to be a follower of Christ. We get this language from **one** verse that Paul wrote to the Corinthian church in I Corinthians 15:31, *I affirm, brethren, by the boasting in you which I have in Christs Jesus our Lord, I die daily.* In the context, Paul also says in verse 30; *Why are we also in danger every hour*. Or in other words, I am in harm's way every day and willing to be slain for the Gospel. This is why many of our modern translations say, *I face death every day*. Also, read the whole chapter and you will see what he was saying, as well as Romans 8:36 that tells us, *for your sake we are being put to death all day long.* Paul also tells us in Romans 6:3, *Or do you not know that all of us who have been baptized into Christ Jesus, have been baptized into His death*? Romans 6:6, *Knowing this, that our old self WAS crucified with Him, in order that our body of sin might be done away with, so that we would no longer be* *slaves to sin.* Also, in Galatians 2:20, *I HAVE BEEN crucified with Christ, and I no longer live, but Christ lives in me, the life I now live in this body, I live by the faith of the Son of God, who loved me and gave His life for me.* Finally, Romans 6:10, *For the death that He died, He died to sin once for all; and the life He now lives, He lives to God.*

As a believer, we have already died, and our lives are not our own, for we have been purchased with a price, and our lives are now hidden with Christ, for when He died we died with Him. So, stop trying to do a bunch of religious gymnastics and jumping thru hoops or trying to die to self which is simply not a New Covenant idea. Paul said his life was being threatened every day, but that does not mean we now beat ourselves or self-flagellate in order to be more spiritual. That was not Paul's intent and with everything else he taught, he would be horrified at the notion. So. stop trying to die, and reckon yourself already dead to sin, alive to Christ and enjoy the eternal life that He now placed in you by His finished work.

Myth #65
Christians are sinners saved by grace.

Many of us have probably heard this in either a sermon or in conversation with Christians, "I am just a sinner saved by grace". Now most understand what someone is saying when they say this, because what most mean is that they still struggle with certain sins, works of their flesh and walking in the Spirit. The problem is, this statement is absolutely not true of ANY Christian. We are no longer a sinner because that infers nature as in identity; we have now become the righteousness of God in Christ Jesus (2 Cor 5:21). So, we are no longer 'sinners' even though we may sin, because a Christian can commit a sin, but that does not change their righteous standing before God or their nature. What we should say is, "I was a sinner, but now saved by grace." We have now become a saint; holy, righteous, whole, and complete. What is true of Jesus is now true of us.

Now realize, this doesn't mean we are free to run around and sin. Sin still has consequences and still leads to death and destruction in our lives. Sowing and reaping are something that effects us in this life positively and negatively. Sin makes us stupid and opens the door to the enemy to reap destruction in our lives, so don't sin! However, if and when you do, it does not change your nature as a son of God and a new creation in Christ Jesus. *For if by the transgression of the one, death reigned through the one, much more those who receive the abundance of grace and of the gift of righteousness will reign in life through the one, Jesus Christ. (*Romans 5:17). The apostle John also tells us, *Because as He is, so also are we in this world.* (I John 4:17) or as other translations say, *We are just like Him on the Earth.*

We need to say what God says about us in Christ Jesus, because righteousness is a gift that cannot be earned or worked for (Rom 10:3-4). Here is a simple example; if an unrighteous person or someone who has not received the gift of righteousness by faith does a righteous deed, does that make them righteous? In the same manner, when a righteous person or someone who has received the gift of righteousness by faith does an unrighteous deed or act, does that make them unrighteous? No in either case, because no amount of righteous deeds makes someone righteous who has not been made righteous by faith, just as well as unrighteous deeds do not make a righteous person unrighteous. So, we are NOT sinners saved by grace, but we are son's and saints who are completely forgiven and loved by their Father

Myth #66

Acts 1:8 is telling us that the Holy Spirit empowers us, so we are not afraid to Knock on our neighbor's door and witness about Jesus.

Let's start by looking at the whole verse at Acts 1:8, *But you will receive power when the Holy Spirit has come upon you; and you shall be my witness' in Jerusalem, Judea, Samaria, and even to the remotest part of the Earth.* Now when we look at this passage at face value it looks like Jesus is simply saying He will empower us to share the gospel around the World. This no doubt is part of it, but not what this original text was focusing on.

The word witness in the Greek language is 'Martus' which is where we get our word martyr from, and means witness, martyr, and recorder. In context Jesus is speaking to His apostles and not the whole church, even though it is applicable to us still today, and He is telling them that He is going to empower them to witness of His martyrdom and be martyred themselves.

Every apostle except John was slain for their testimony and, some like Thomas, as far away as India, which would qualify as the far reaches of the Earth. Also, many today around the World are still being martyred for their faith and the Holy Spirit empowers them to withstand it.

Let's be honest, do we really need the power of the Holy Spirit to tell our neighbor about the lover of our soul and Savior who has transformed our lives? That's what I was raised to think, yet we have Jehovah's witness' and Mormon's who do not claim the power of the Spirit and they do a way better job than most Christians in talking to their neighbors. Jesus was telling them that this power would allow them to look death in the eye and like Peter say, "Crucify me upside down" or like many Christians, when being fed to the lions in Rome, were said to be forgiving the crowd and singing songs of worship while being torn apart.

It's amazing how many people feel they need a special touch to simply live out their relationship with God in the marketplace daily. When we receive Christ, He and the Godhead come to live in us, and sharing that with others is simply an overflow of that union. However, if I am living in Syria or Iraq or most of the middle East and know that just admitting I am a believer could get me beheaded, that is something I need to be empowered to live, because I could be martyred for that witness.

This is why we have been empowered by the Spirit, to take this Kingdom Good News to the far reaches of the Earth and not just willing to live for Christ, but willing and empowered to die for Him.

Myth #67
God had to enlarge hell to fit more human sinners.

This is a statement that many have heard in sermons and teachings through the years that is not completely incorrect depending on the translation, but when you study the context and the original Hebrew it takes on a very different meaning. We get this from Isaiah 5:14, *Therefore sheol (hell in KJV) has enlarged its throat and opened its mouth without measure; And Jerusalem's splendor, her multitude, her din of revelry and her jubilant within her, descend into it.* (NASB) This is also THE ONLY time the Scriptures even come close to saying the above myth.

The first thing that proper hermeneutics (the art of interpretation) teaches us is, you cannot just pull verses out of their surrounding context to build doctrine. When you read Isaiah 1-5 they are speaking to the destruction of Jerusalem in judgement by foreign armies and invaders, as well as from within, thru rebelling against God. Isaiah 1:7, *Your land is desolate, your cities are burned with fire, your fields—strangers are devouring them in your presence; It is desolation, as overthrown by strangers.* Also, Isaiah chapter 3:25, *Your men will fall by the sword, and your mighty ones in battle".*

The well-respected commentator and expositor Gill says it like this, "Therefore hell hath enlarged herself; that is, the grave, to receive the dead which die with famine and thirst; signifying that the number of the dead would be so great, that the common burying places would not be sufficient to hold them; but additions must be made to them; or some vast prodigious pit must be dug, capable of receiving them; like Tophet, deep and large: for 'she hath enlarged her soul'.

When you study other translations only a few use the word 'hell' most either use the Hebrew word 'sheol' or 'grave and death'. The reason is, the word translated as 'hell' in Hebrew is the grave, the pit, the underworld, and death. As Gill said above, all Isaiah is saying is, there is a massive battle and war coming, and the graves are going to have to be larger than normal because of all the death and destruction brought on by Israel's rebellious ways.

The ancient Israelite's as well as most cultures in the days of the Old Testament writings viewed the afterlife as simply falling asleep with your fathers. They had little to no concept of Heaven and hell, the way many of us in the West have been taught, and the idea of eternal torment was not introduced until the

New Testament era. You will find no mention of afterlife torment under the law; the wages of sin was simply; Death.

Now this does not mean that there is not a place (places) called hell in many of our translations, but in this instance in Isaiah, it is not referring to God having to expand an eternal torture chamber to fit more sinners into. It is simply - the grave is opening to accept more dead.

Myth #68
Hell is a place that is void of God's presence.

If you have been around church or Christians very long you have no doubt heard the above said. However, when you try to find Scripture for it, the opposite seems to be of more truth. The Psalmist David tells us in Psalm 139: 7-8, *Where can I go from your Spirit? Or where can I flee from your presence? If I ascend to Heaven, You are there; if I make my bed in hell (sheol=grave) behold, you are there.* David seems to more than imply that Hell is a place where God's presence is, and that He will come to wherever you run to, regardless of height or depth.

The apostle Paul also tells us in Ephesians 4:6, *One God and Father of all, who is over all, through all, and in all.* Also, in Colossians 1:15-17, *He is the image of the invisible God, the firstborn over all creation. For by Him ALL things were created, both in the Heaven and on the Earth, visible and invisible, whether thrones or dominions or rulers or authorities--all things have been created through Him and for Him. He is before all things, and in Him ALL things hold together.*

The apostle John also puts it like this in

his Gospel, John 1:2-3, *He was in the beginning with God. All things came into being through Him, and apart from Him nothing came into being that has come into being.* Then Hebrews 1:3, *And He is the radiance of His glory and the exact representation of His nature and upholds all tings by the word of His power. When He had made purification of sins, He sat down at the right hand of the Majesty on high.*

    The main verse that most use for this myth is found in 2 Thessalonians 1:9, *these will pay the penalty of eternal destruction, away from the presence of the Lord and from the glory of His power* (NASB). The NIV and a few others interpret this as being punished and shut out or forever separated from the presence of the Lord. Now, to follow right interpretation, we also can't have one verse that throws out a bunch of others, especially New Covenant ones that say the opposite; we must look at the original language and other interpretations. My 'go to' for a more literal translation is the YLT the Young's Literal Translation, and this is how he interprets it, *who shall suffer justice, destruction - age-enduring, from the face of the Lord, and from the glory of His strength"* This shows that it is not FOREVER, and it does have some kind of ending; and this destruction comes from the presence of the Lord.

Then, a big monkey wrench gets thrown in when you read Revelation 14:10, *he also, will drink the wine of the wrath of God, which is mixed in full strength in the cup of His anger; and he will be tormented with fire and brimstone in the PRESENCE OF THE HOLY ANGELS AND THE LAMB"*. WAIT; WHAT?

There are many verses that show that nothing exists outside of God's all encompassing presence. If hell was a place that God was not, then hell would be a God to itself for it would have to uphold and sustain itself, and we do not have any Scripture for that. Also, regardless of which of the 3 main views you embrace, when it comes to hell and the afterlife, the idea of God's presence being there would make it either more tormenting by knowing that you can sense His love and His presence, or more redemptive and restorative, or destructive depending on your view. Just know that there is no place that He is not, and His presence is even in the dark places we find ourselves in,

Myth 69

The Old Covenant law is broken up into three sections in Scripture; Moral Law, Ceremonial Law, and Judicial Law.

This is something that gets taught quite often to always have Christians keeping the law in some form. Many teachers and leaders will say, "We as Christians are not under the ceremonial laws of the old covenant, but we are still under the moral laws of the Ten Commandments." The first question should be which ten commandments, which I covered in Myth 61? Then, where in Scripture does it teach this? There is no Scriptural evidence or differentiation for this distinction.

The apostle Paul would beg to differ, He wrote that *we are not under law, but under grace*, Romans 6:14. He also called the law of Moses *the ministry of death and condemnation written on stones* (2 Corinthians 3:7 & 9). Paul gives no distinction of the law being broken up into sections, and when you study this you find that it is a human construct to try and explain to Jews as well as to Gentile Christians why they should still keep the ten commandments.

Then, Peter in Acts 15:10-11 says that putting anyone under the law in the New Covenant is tempting God. The apostle James in his Epistle tells us that the law is an ALL or NOTHING type of thing, for if you are going to keep it then you have to keep all of it. James 2:10, *For whoever keeps the whole law and yet stumbles at just one point is guilty of breaking ALL of it.* This is not just speaking of the big TEN but the whole of the law with no differentiation.

Jesus tells us that we are given one commandment in the New Covenant and that is to love as He loved, John 13:34. James also called it a royal law and the law of liberty, James 2:8 & 12, *If however, you are fulfilling the royal law according to the Scripture, 'You Shall Love Your Neighbor as Yourself,' you are doing well. 12) So, speak and so act as those who are to be judged by the law of liberty.* Then Paul in Romans 8:2, calls it the law of life in Christ Jesus. *For the law of the Spirit of life in Christ Jesus has set you free from the law of sin and of death.*

Now we can still learn from those laws and there are wise statutes and principles in many of them, along with some types and shadows of Christ, but we are not obligated to keep them, period. Matter of fact, no one for the last nearly 2000 years has been born under law, because it has been made obsolete Hebrews 8:13, *When He said, 'a new covenant'*

He has made the first obsolete. But whatever is becoming obsolete and growing old is ready to disappear; And been abolished at the cross, Ephesians 2:15, *by abolishing in His flesh the enmity, which is the Law of commandments contained in ordinances, so that in Himself He might make the two into one new man, thus establishing peace.* So, if it helps you to distinguish them to understand them, then I do not see any problem with that, but don't try to make it a doctrine when it is NOT.

Myth 70
God doesn't send anyone to hell, they send themselves.

I waited till the last one to write this myth, because many of us have said this and believe it, even though there is no Scripture for it. Also, when I have brought this up to people in the past, they get angry rather than think and dialogue. The above statement is a 'go to' saying when a Christian gets asked about hell as an eternal torture chamber. Normally, we get asked the question, "If God is love then why would He create and send anyone to a place of torture forever?" Then, many of us have been taught to say, "God doesn't send anyone to hell they send themselves by rejecting Him.

This may sound good, but the question would then arise, "What about those who have never heard or had a chance to reject Him?" They send themselves to eternal torture through ignorance? Not only does this not make any sense (and Romans 1 does not explain that either) but Jesus is THE ONE who the Father gave all judgement to and He alone has the keys (authority) of death and hell (Hades= grave) so no one can go in or out without His authority. We do not have the authority to send ourselves anywhere eternally, period.

Now we can send ourselves to an early grave (hell) by bad habits and wrong decisions. We can also have confidence that once we have received His love and believed that we have no fear to stand before God on Judgment day (1John 4). So, believing removes any fear and gives us boldness and confidence that we will not have to taste death but have eternal life. However, that does not mean those who do not believe send themselves to hell.

Revelation 20 & 21 actually paint the picture of all the dead standing before God and then being separated and cast into the lake of fire along with death and hell (grave) if you interpret those passages literally, which many do. If that is so, then it is God doing it on Judgement day and not ourselves. Only He has the power to make that kind of judgement. So, if hell gets thrown into the lake of fire than maybe those are two different things, and we probably should take the time to study all of that out, before we start sending people there.

If we are honest we only say this myth because we cannot imagine the God, who is exactly like Jesus, doing this to someone. So, we had to come up with an excuse to make Him look better. An eternal torture chamber is abhorring to us, and we would not wish it on our worst enemy. I have taught for years that if we are more loving and merciful than our God, then maybe our view of Him is wrong.

Jesus taught us to love our enemies, yet we believe that He is going to torture His which would make Him a liar and a hypocrite. Selah!

About the Author

Jamie Englehart is the president/founder of Connect International Ministries based in Bay City, MI. He has traveled all over the world for over 27 years and functions as a Bishop and apostle to many that receive him in that capacity. Jamie is widely sought out for his insight and oversight and serves many as an overseer. His understanding of the Kingdom of God, the New Covenant and the heart of the Father revealed in Christ, is what he is passionate about sharing to his generation and the next. Jamie is married to Wendy Englehart, who is a recording artist, who traveled with him for their first 21 years. They have two children, Brittany Rocha and Brandon Englehart, as well as a son-in-love, Estevan Rocha and a beautiful grand-daughter, Caydence Rocha, who is one of the joys in their lives.

Contact Information

www.connectinternationalministries.com

C.I.M.
P.O Box 188
Bay City, MI 48707

CPSIA information can be obtained
at www.ICGtesting.com
Printed in the USA
LVHW080346150822
725952LV00011B/395